YEAR
R–1

G000124369

The Synthetic Phonics Book

Helen Hadley

Nelson Thornes
a Wolters Kluwer business

Published in 2006 by:
Nelson Thornes Ltd
Delta Place
27 Bath Road
CHELTENHAM
GL53 7TH
United Kingdom

06 07 08 09 10 / 10 9 8 7 6 5 4 3 2 1

A catalogue record for this book is available from the British Library

ISBN 0-7487-9769-6

Page make-up by GreenGate Publishing Services, Tonbridge, Kent

Printed in Great Britain by Ashford Colour Press

Contents

Introduction

Synthetic Phonics

Preface

Classworks *Synthetic Phonics* is a practical programme which teaches the 40+ individual sounds (phonemes) of the English language. It consists of this book and the related *Classworks Synthetic Phonics Photocopiable Readers*, which provide more reading practice, week by week, in a photocopiable form. *Synthetic Phonics* shows children how to blend phonemes to make words. It is designed for use with children from the beginning of their first term in school. It provides a range of learning tasks and activities to develop and reinforce phonic knowledge, which places them securely on the road to effective reading and is totally in line with the latest advice from the government on the effective use of phonics to boost reading success.

A systematic sequence and method is used. Children become familiar with the processes and confusion is minimised. Through the routine of daily lessons and its fast pace, this highly systematic whole-class teaching programme involves children actively in the learning process. They soon come to realise that words written down mean something to the reader – and that they are fast becoming readers themselves.

What is synthetic phonics and why does it work?

Synthetic phonics is a single, effective word-identification strategy. It is a highly structured technique for teaching reading which has been proved to be extremely effective. The term 'synthetic' comes from the verb 'to synthesise' (to combine), i.e. the reader combines the sounds in a word and so is able to read that word. It is vital that this programme is used *before* any other technique or method is introduced.

Do not dip into this programme. Yes, this is a programme, not a resource to use among other methods of teaching reading. You must use it solely, totally, without deviating to any other method. To make this system work you need to be totally committed to synthetic phonics. If you are, you will give your children a flying start along the road to reading.

By starting this programme at the beginning of their first term in school, children are well on their way to becoming readers by the end of that first term. Children don't think it is boring, they enjoy 'cracking' the reading code. It increases their listening and concentration skills, which has pay-offs in all other areas of learning. It also builds up their confidence and self-esteem as they become aware of how their reading skills are growing.

Children begin using direct letter–sound correspondence from Day 1 and blending letters to form words from Day 2. The quick pace of teaching letter–sound correspondence is such that children can use the knowledge to read and spell regular words immediately. They are soon able to apply their learning to unknown words as they progress along the path to becoming a reader. Once the programme has been completed, other reading strategies can be introduced.

This book will provide you with a simple, low-cost approach to synthetic phonics in your school, and contains all you need to teach your children to read.

The main features are as follows:

- the synthetic phonics method is one which is used completely on its own, *not* alongside any other reading strategies;

- it systematically teaches the different forms of the 40+ phonemes in the English language in a direct, structured programme;
- children are taught to blend the letters from Week 1 of Term 1 at school, so that they read confidently from the start;
- this rapid, intensive programme ensures that *all* children keep up;
- it is a fast-paced daily programme with highly systematic whole-class teaching that involves children actively in the learning process;
- its multi-sensory approach teaches both reading and writing at the same time;
- once children know the phonics taught in this programme, they are able to comprehend what they are reading and approach unknown words;
- the majority of English words are phonically structured. This programme gives children the skills to build many of these words.

There is now a wealth of research evidence to show that:

- starting from Day 1, with an effective synthetic phonics programme, children take off faster and more confidently into reading than those who do not use synthetic phonics;
- boys and girls make equal progress;
- it is an efficient programme which works with a higher percentage of the school population than the usual methods of teaching reading;
- synthetic phonics is a single, extremely effective word-identification strategy that really works.

Why?

- It is a simple, practical, straightforward method of teaching reading and writing.
- Children do not have to work out which strategy to use to identify a word.
- They learn to read and write one new letter or letter cluster at a time.
- Each new letter is used to make words with letters previously learnt.
- Children begin building words and phrases from Week 1.
- They begin reading and building sentences from Week 2.
- They begin reading stories from Week 3.
- Children read only material built from the letters they have learnt – there is no guessing, so they do not find reading difficult.
- No expensive stocks of apparatus or equipment are required.
- And – most importantly – no one gets left behind.

In order to be successful with synthetic phonics it is essential that you understand and follow the golden rules of synthetic phonics teaching. These are outlined on page viii.

What next?

Once the programme is completed the children will know 40+ phonemes of our language and they will be secure in blending these phonemes to form words. They will be able to build so many words that they can make sensible guesses at unknown words through this knowledge and through the context of what they are reading. The emphasis next needs to be placed on understanding what they read and using that knowledge. More complex phonemic structures such as vowel digraphs with /r/ – 'fair', 'fear' etc., double consonants in the middle of words – 'rabbit', 'drummer' etc., /er/ and /y/ endings – 'robber', 'dummy' etc., can be introduced, along with the many sight words that are an important part of the English language.

Children who have some reading ability

Children who come to school with some reading ability generally read by sight but do not necessarily know how words are built. Learning the structure of words and how to blend them helps them to understand how words are formed and how to tackle unfamiliar words. It reinforces their knowledge and gives them a much firmer basis for further learning. If they are really good readers, working with slow learners reinforces their own language learning and fills in gaps they may not have realised were there.

Key features of the programme

Synthetic phonics is for children at the beginning of their first year of schooling. It is taught *on its own* through a carefully structured, intensive programme. It is *not mixed with other methods* and it is not desirable to use reading books from schemes that do not follow this strict phonic progression. (For this reason, the accompanying *Classworks Synthetic Phonics Photocopiable Readers* will be found extremely useful in providing extra reading practice during this intensive programme.) The method involves teaching letters very rapidly in a way that is designed to capture children's attention.

The key features are as follows:

1 **The letters are taught in a specific and logical order from the first week of schooling for a half-hour period every day and reinforced at odd moments during the day.**

- Children learn the different forms of the 40+ phonemes, made by single letters or small groups of letters.
- With this programme, children learn to recognise, sound out and write letters at the rate of four a week. They learn quickly how to read words, blend letters to make words, and spell the words they need to write.

2 **Children are taught to read by putting the learnt letters together and blending them to make simple, monosyllabic words.**

- They start with the simplest letter-to-sound correspondences using groups of letters from which the maximum number of words can be built.
- Letters are taught in the initial, middle and final positions in words.
- Consonant blends are not taught explicitly, but consonant and vowel digraphs are. Digraphs are phonemes (single sounds) represented by two letters e.g. /sh/, /ai/, /ou/.

3 **Letter sounds, blending and letter formation are taught at the same time.**

- Four letters, digraphs or long vowel sounds are learnt each week, one per day, with a review day on the last day of the week.
- The letters are grouped in such a way that word building begins from Day 2.
- The words selected for the worksheets are for their ease of blending. They show the day's letter in different positions in the words and are chosen from words in common usage.
- Only lower-case letters are used at this stage (not capital letters) so that children learn only one letter shape to represent a letter. Capital letters can be introduced once the programme has been completed.

4 **The correct pronunciation of letters is vital to the success of this programme.**

- 'Pure' sounds, those without a 'schwa' ending, are essential, for example a light hiss for /s/ not /suh/, /mmm/ for /m/ not /muh/. Letter names must not be used at this stage.

5 **Blending is important from the beginning and is vital to the success of this programme.**

- When blending letters to make words, children need to hold on to one sound and then move on to the next without a break so the letters almost blend themselves into the word – saaaaaaat. This is detailed in each week's lesson plan.

6 **Only one sight word a week is introduced from Week 3.**

- Commencing from Week 3 one high-frequency sight word a week is introduced. These words are referred to as 'star words' – see page 3.

7 **Learning to write is an integral part of this programme.**

- Children are taught how to write each letter as they learn its sound, so that one is an integral part of and reinforces the other.
- Being taught the correct letter formation from the beginning enables children to develop good, clear handwriting.
- Children learn to say a word that they want to write slowly, e.g. mmmaaann. Hearing its phonemes /m/ /a/ /n/, they are able to write the grapheme for each phoneme and so write the word.

8 **There is a clear fifteen-week programme.**

- There is a clear programme for teaching the basics that can be covered in one term. You may prefer to consolidate the first term's learning in the last two weeks of term and transfer the remaining few weeks of the programme to the next term.
- It details what is to be taught every day. See 'the sequence for teaching letters', page 8.

9 **Each day's work is clearly laid out with lesson notes to accompany each week's photocopiable pages. There is also a review page for the end of each week.**

- This photocopiable material helps children to form the new letter's shape correctly, to pick out the letter from amongst others, and to use it with letters previously learnt to form words.
- Once children have learnt the letters for that week, a number of activities and worksheets are provided to reinforce this synthetic phonic method of teaching reading and to set children firmly on the path towards becoming fluent readers. *Classworks Synthetic Phonics Photocopiable Readers* can be used at this point to provide lots more practice and take-home material.

10 **Letter sheets, letter fans, and word lists are provided which contain words made from the letters learnt to date.**

- The letter sheets can be photocopied onto card. They have the letters placed at the left-hand edge of each card so that they can be pushed together to form words. See pages 19–23.
- Letter fans can also be copied onto cards. Use split pins to hold the letter fans together so that they can be fanned out to build words – letters can be added to a word, taken away, reversed (e.g. 'pat' – 'tap') and so on, yet they can be held in one hand.

- Other activities are provided which can be photocopied to reinforce the letters learnt and to assist word building. These can be used as a whole-class activity or in smaller groups with the classroom assistant.
- Again, *Classworks Synthetic Phonics Readers* will provide more practice in phonic skills.

11. **The approach involves whole-class teaching.**

- This programme employs whole-class teaching. It is essential to keep the whole class together.
- Refresh the letter learnt that day at odd moments during the day with the whole class.
- Any children who have difficulty keeping up must have a reinforcement session with you or the classroom assistant later that day to ensure they are ready to move on the following day.

Ten golden rules for success with synthetic phonics

Here we have set down briefly the keys to success with this method.

1 Keep the progress of the whole class together – it is essential that slower-learning children are given extra sessions the same day to ensure they keep up.

2 Reinforce the day's new letter whenever you have an odd moment during the day.

3 Use only the letter's sound, not its name.

4 Do not add the schwa sound (/uh/ or /er/) to a letter, use only its pure sound.

5 Do not put one letter with another which affects its pure sound until that combination is taught, e.g. teach blending /r/ with /a/ (as in 'ran') in Week 2 but not /a/ with /r/ (as in 'car') until the /ar/ phoneme has been taught in Week 14.

6 Begin to build known letters into words from Day 2.

7 Read sentences from the end of Week 2.

8 Learn to write each letter mirror-fashion yourself so you can face children when demonstrating the letter and can see whether they form it correctly.

9 Stand up facing your class and write the letter to be learnt as big as you can using a large, across-the-body movement.

10 Do not introduce any other method of teaching reading until this programme has been completed.

The Programme

About the programme

In this programme you are provided with a sequence for teaching letter sounds and a lesson plan for each of the fifteen weeks of the programme. It details the way to teach the phonemes and graphemes of each letter and provides activities to support and reinforce that learning.

The programme is carefully and deliberately thought through. It is structured in such a way that children acquire accurate knowledge of reading skills in the shortest possible time. Synthetic phonics is a single learning strategy so it is vitally important that no other techniques for teaching reading or letter names be introduced until the programme is completed. Every child should take part in the programme irrespective of their ability; it is a whole-class approach to learning to read.

The programme is in three stages: Stage 1 is the learning and blending of single letters into one syllable words, Stage 2 deals with consonant digraphs, and Stage 3 with long vowels and vowel digraphs.

Children need to be able to use letters freely and easily, so each day starts with a ten-minute, fast-paced review of letters learnt to date. This is followed by teaching the day's new letter. Although you will work through the daily review more quickly in Week 1, still follow the steps of its structure. Learning is fostered when the learner has the opportunity to practise their newly acquired information so that the strategies and techniques they learn at one session are brought to the next lesson, this way learning is reinforced and made more efficient.

Before you start, tell children what they are going to learn and why. Tell them which phoneme they are going to learn that day and show them how it can be added to those they already know. By teaching the phonemes one at a time, the letters become like building blocks on which other letters and words can be built.

Each week of the fifteen-week programme is carefully explained. A lesson plan is provided for each week, a page of work supplied to provide children with practice for the letter or digraph taught each day, and a review page for each Friday. The review page is followed by activities which support the letters taught so far. They are for use when children have learnt that week's letters, i.e. after Thursday's lesson and on Friday. Children must know one week's sounds before going on to those of the following week. Keeping the class together is essential, so ensure that slower learners have extra practice each day so they can keep up.

Learning the pure sound for each letter is an essential element of this programme, as is learning to blend letters, writing the shape and spelling words. These are detailed overleaf, so please read them carefully.

Saying the sound of the letters

Here is the order for teaching the letters and making the sound of those letters:

Week 1	vowel **a**	+	front of mouth sounds	**n t s**
Week 2	vowel **i**	+	front of mouth sounds	**d l r**
Week 3	vowel **e**	+	lip sounds	**p m f**
Week 4	vowel **o**	+	back of throat sounds	**c g h**
Week 5	vowel **u**	+	lip sounds	**b v w**
Week 6			back of mouth sounds	**k y**
			and front of mouth sounds	**j z**

- It is vital that children learn to say the sound of a letter without a schwa ending, i.e. a short /t/ not lengthened into /tuh/ or /ter/.
- When you introduce a consonant, say the letter and then ask children to repeat it. Ask them what helps them say the letter – their lips, their tongue, their throat? For tip-of-the-tongue sounds or lip sounds, ask them to put the palm of one hand close to their mouths – what do they feel? For back-of-the-throat sounds they hold the neck behind the jaw between the thumb and fingers to feel the sound being made.
- Ask them to repeat the letters loudly, softly, in a high voice, and in a low one.
- Say a three-lettered word, made from letters learned to date, and ask children which sound it begins with, which it ends with, which sound is in the middle (in that order, because that takes them from the easiest sound to hear to the most difficult).
- Ask the children to give you words which begin with the same sound, or have the same sound at the end or in the middle. If they give you a non-real word, ask them if they know what the word means. If they do not know its meaning (perhaps they were just guessing) tell them that it was good try, but it was not a real word. Can they think of another word?

Blending letters together to make words

Children need to learn how to blend letters together, to run one into another, to form words for both reading and writing. This begins on Day 2 once they have learnt the two letters.

- Using the letter sheets or letter fans, show or write the first letter of a word, e.g. 'at'.
- Say its first letter /a/ slowly as you write it or run your finger underneath it, add the second letter /t/ and sound the word – aaat.
- Say the word several times, running your finger under the word.
- Say it more quickly each time until the word is said in its normal way.
- Remove the word, ask children to write /a/, then /t/, then to write the whole word.
- At the end of Week 2 they can begin to write pairs of words and short phrases at your dictation, e.g. 'a pan'; 'a rat in a tin'. Take your time, do not rush it.
- Send home the week's zigzag book on a Friday for children to read to their parents to keep them appraised of what their child is learning and the progress being made.
- From the end of Week 3, also send home a minute track each Friday for children to practise speed reading and word recognition daily with their parents.

Writing

Children are taught to write using graphemes in a simple form. They learn a style similar to the letters which appear in many books for the young, as well as in their school environment. This enables children to recognise words in the world around them and so put their learning into practice. First they are taught to write a really huge letter in front of them crossing the body line incorporating both the right and the left side of the body. This cross-body movement engages both sides of the brain. Next children write it in the air, and then feel the movement of their finger writing it on the table before picking up a pencil or crayon and starting to write it on paper. Each day's activity page reinforces the correct movement to shape the letter.

Once the programme has been completed, children will be ready to take on other writing strategies leading to joined writing. Because they have learnt the basic shape of a letter, the joining of letters will follow quite quickly but the letters will retain a good shape.

Spelling

Children need to say the word they want to write slowly, so they can identify the different phonemes in the word. They then say the phonemes in turn and write the grapheme for each phoneme to produce the written word. If a child writes a word phonetically, e.g. 'bak' instead of 'back' before they have learnt the appropriate consonant digraph – accept it without comment. They will learn the correct spelling when they reach that stage.

Star words

Star words are sight words; words that have to be learnt by the look of them not by blending their letters. They are called star words because they are special, different from the words they are learning to build, and always appear within this symbol:

They are put in a star to separate them from phonemically built words, to make them look different and for children to recognise that they are different.

Sight words are often called 'funny' or 'tricky' words because they are irregular and do not fit any learned pattern. Only a very few of the common ones used in everyday language are taught in this programme. They are taught in an order which will allow children to use them in their reading and writing straight away.

- Only one star word is taught each week from Week 3.
- Talk about the word and its usage.
- Photocopy the large star in the Teacher Resources section, write the week's sight word on it, use it as a flash card and keep it pinned up where it can be seen and used during the day, e.g. while lining up at the door, between one lesson and the next, when sitting down for story time.
- Once three or more have been learnt, use them in flash cards activities.

Order for teaching star words:

Week	3	4	5	6	7	8	9	10	11	12	13	14	15
Star word	I	my	the	to	of	was	for	he	we	she	said	they	me

Daily review

From the beginning of Week 2 start each day with this ten-minute revision session. It will remind children of letters they have already learnt and prepare them for the day's new letter.

Preparation:

- Make large letters, one per A4 sheet.
- Laminate or mount on card, punch holes in the top and make a loop to hang them by.
- Photocopy letters and letter fans for word building. Cut out each letter and laminate or mount on card.
- Make flash cards of words using known letter sounds and laminate or mount on card. Write the word on both sides so you can also see the word you are holding up. You will need at least two copies of letters learnt in the first weeks, after that, experience will tell you how many you need.

Note: a list of words for each of the three stages of this programme is on pages 11–13.

Daily sessions – 10 minutes

- Sit the children in front of you.
- Have to hand the large letter cards, letter fans for word building and blending, and the flash cards you have created.

  1 Letter practice – 2 minutes

  - Using known letter sounds, hold up each letter card in turn. You say its sound; children repeat.
  - Do this several times, showing the cards faster each time.
  - Ensure only pure sounds are used.

  2 Using the letter sounds – 2 minutes

  - Show a letter, say its sound and say a word that begins with the sound – you say; they repeat: /a/ – 'ant'.
  - You show a letter; they give you a word beginning with its sound.
  - Children say words and names that begin with the new sound.

  3 Blending the sounds to make words – 2 minutes

  - Hold up known words one after the other to make a word, e.g. 'pat'. You say the word 'pat'; next say each sound clearly, /p/ /a/ /t/ – then say the whole word again, 'pat'. Do this with words made from known letters.
  - Children repeat the word, the letter sounds, and then say the word again.
  - Ensure that only pure sounds are used.

  4 Flash cards – 2 minutes

  - Using the words you have made from the Friday review pages as a pack of flash cards, hold them up one by one, gradually getting faster as you repeat your way through the pack.
  - Make flash cards using a selection from the word lists on pages 11–13.

5 Making words – 2 minutes

- Give letter cards to some of the children. Give to different children each time, so all have a chance to participate as well as watching to see whether the word is formed correctly.
- Say a known word or phrase.
- Children with a letter from that word or phrase hold it up and you ask one of them to come out and show their letter. Do this for each letter. The children at the front must put themselves in the right order to form the word or phrase.
- Children watching say whether the letters are held in the right order and whether the word is correct.
- You point to the letters in turn. Children say the letters, then the word.

Now the children have been reminded of what they already know, they are ready to learn the day's letter.

Games and activities

In addition to the daily activity pages, a selection of the games and activities listed below is included with each week's lesson plan. These can be used at the end of each week, once children have learnt that week's sounds. The activities are introduced gradually, then developed and extended through the following weeks.

Class activities

Use letter cards, letter fans and your own flash cards to support the daily review activities.

Letter fan activities
- Cut out the letter fans from pages 14–18 and mount on card. It will be helpful to have at least two copies of each fan, especially in the first few weeks.
- Use the fans to demonstrate, build and manipulate letters and words.
- Fans can be held together with split pins and opened out gradually or fanned forwards or backwards while held in one hand.
- Hold up the letters for a word, e.g. /e/, /n/, /t/, say the real word – 'net' and ask a child to put the letters in the right order.
- Hold up a fan with two letters, e.g. /a/, /n/; ask the children which letter must be added to make the word 'and'.

Other activities include:

- adding letters: a, an, pan, pant, pants
- deleting letters: stand, sand, and, an
- reversing words: tap – pat; net – ten
- inserting letters: set – sent; pat – pant
- combining words: hat + pin = hatpin

Individual activities

These activities can be used at other times during the day to reinforce letters being learnt.

Matching sounds and pictures – Stage 1
- Say the letter sounds down the centre of the page.
- Say what is in each picture.
- Draw a line to join the correct letter to its picture.

Complete the words for the pictures – Stage 2
- Say the consonant clusters down the centre of the page.
- Say what is in each picture.
- Write the missing letter clusters for each picture.

Building words for pictures – Stage 3
- Say the vowel digraphs down the centre of the page.
- Say what is in each picture.
- Use the vowel digraphs and other consonants to complete the words.

Find the right word – Stages 2 and 3
- Say what is in the picture, read all three words and then circle the right word.

Zigzag books – Stages 1, 2 and 3

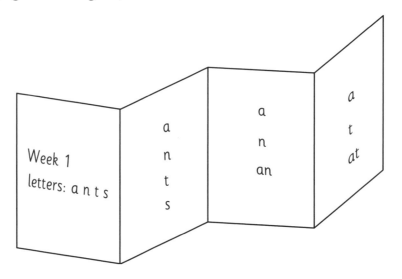

- Prepare one for each child to take home at the end of each week from Week 1.
- Fold horizontally across the dotted line in the middle.
- Fold inwards down the middle and turn back the outer sections to form a zigzag.
- The zigzag book for the week should go home every Friday.

Minute tracks
- At the end of each week (from Week 3) send the appropriate page home.
- Ask parents to time their child reading the word track and stop when one minute is up.
- The child then colours in the word reached when one minute is up.
- This is their target to beat the next time.
- Ask parents to do this with them two or three times every day.
- The object is to complete the track in one minute by the end of the week.

Classworks Synthetic Phonics Photocopiable Readers

The companion book to *Classworks: The Synthetic Phonics Book* contains additional reinforcement reading material for use from Week 3. It provides further texts for each week which reinforce the letters and words learnt to date. These pages can be photocopied for use in school and also taken home for children to read to their parents.

Targets to reach

By the end of Stage 1 children must:

- have secure knowledge of letter–sound correspondence;
- confidently use phoneme–grapheme correspondence;
- recognise the terms: first   last   middle;
- be able to read, write and spell simple monosyllabic words;
- begin to blend two pure consonants at the beginning of one syllable, e.g. /sp/, /tr/;
- use correct direction and orientation when forming letters;
- read and spell these sight words: I, my, the, to.

By the end of Stage 2 children should also be able to:

- recognise and use consonant clusters;
- read, write and spell one-syllable words using consonant clusters;
- read, write and spell these sight words: of, was, for.

By the end of Stage 3 children should also be able to:

- recognise and use long vowel sounds and vowel digraphs;
- read, write and spell one-syllable words using long vowel sounds, vowel digraphs and letter clusters;
- read, write and spell these sight words: he, we, she, said, they, me.

The classroom assistant

If you have a classroom assistant or helper they need to work alongside you. They need to watch and listen to the way the day's letter is taught in the morning session, so that the same procedure can be followed when they repeat it later in the day with children who are slower learners. This will ensure that such children are ready to move on with the rest of the class the next day. They can also work with small groups of children using both the class and individual activities on pages 5–6.

Parental involvement

Parents need to know what their children are learning in school and how they can help. Hold a meeting to explain the programme to them and their role in their child's learning to read. Explain how children learn the sounds and how to pronounce them. Tell them about the zigzag books and the minute tracks which children will bring home, and their purpose. These activities are not a one-off but an everyday event, two or three times a day.

Once their children have completed this programme and mastered the sounds and rules for blending these sounds, they can concentrate on what they read, not how to read it. Remind them to praise their children, to tell them what is good about what they have done, and to be positive in their approach. This way they will really help their child learn to read and so become a good reader at an early age.

Sequence for teaching letters

Stage 1 — Pure consonants and short vowel sounds

Stage 2 — Consonant digraphs plus tch and x (ks) · Long vowel sounds

Stage 3 — Vowel digraphs · Vowels with r and other vowel forms

Weeks	1	2	3	4	5	6	7	8	9	10	11	12	13	14	15
Letter recognition:	a t n s	i d l r	e p m f	o c g h	u b v w	k y j z	ch sh th tch	ck ss ll ff	qu ng nk x	a-e i-e o-e u-e	ee ai ay oo (moo)	oa oi/oy ou ow (owl)	ea oo (book) aw ow (glow)	ar ir or ur	er ight y ew
working with letter shapes, sounding out, flash cards	Review	Review	Review	Review	Review	Review	Review	Review	Review	Review	Review	Review	Review	Review	Review

Blending

Stage 1 (weeks 1–6):
- Listening to sounds
- Saying letters both loudly and softly, high voice and low voice
- Blending sounds to make words
- Sounding out letters in a word
- Making up simple words and sentences
- Writing story sentences

Stage 2 (weeks 7–9):
- A digraph is two letters representing one phoneme
- Blend short sounds with digraphs to make words
- Use in writing stories

From week 10:
- Learn long vowel sounds
- Blend with simple consonants to form words
- Blend with digraphs to form words
- Use in writing stories and writing letters home

Letter formation
- Large across the body movements
- Air and finger tracing movements on the table
- Writing letters with crayons and pencils
- Tracing letters
- Note: letters are written as closely as possible to the way they appear in children's books – NOT joined

| Sight words: a few common ones only | | | I | my | the | to | of | was | for | he | we | she | said | they | me |

8

Checklist

Dates _____ _____ _____ _____

Pupil's name   **Class**

The pupil reads the word first and then says the sound.
Tick for correct response.

Single sounds

ant	a ___	tap	t ___	net	n ___	sit	s ___
in	i ___	dip	d ___	lap	l ___	rat	r ___
egg	e ___	pip	p ___	man	m ___	fit	f ___
on	o ___	cat	c ___	gap	g ___	hat	h ___
up	u ___	bun	b ___	vat	v ___	wet	w ___
kit	k ___	yet	y ___	jam	j ___	zip	z ___

Consonant clusters

chat	ch ___	shin	sh ___	thin	th ___	hatch	tch ___
wick	ck ___	miss	ss ___	sell	ll ___	fluff	ff ___
quit	qu ___	bang	ng ___	ink	nk ___	cox	x ___

Long vowel sounds and digraphs

lane	long a ___	wine	long i ___	hose	long o ___	cute	long u ___
keep	ee ___	rain	ai ___	pay	ay ___	moo	oo ___
soak	oa ___	toil	oi ___	shout	ou ___	owl	ow ___
beat	ea ___	took	oo ___	law	aw ___	glow	ow ___
bar	ar ___	skirt	ir ___	for	or ___	fur	ur ___
her	er ___	sight	ight ___	by	y ___	threw	ew ___

Star words

I	___	my	___	the	___	to	___
of	___	was	___	for	___	he	___
we	___	she	___	said	___	they	___
me	___						

Dear Parent,

Almost everything your child does and learns to do is based on being able to read – to make progress in every subject at school, to read instructions, to read for information, even to complete forms such as their tax return in later life, they need to be able to read.

This term your child is being taught to read by a method called synthetic phonics. With this method they learn the pure sound of four letters a week and how to synthesise (blend) them to make words.

From the first week, on a Friday, your child will bring home a small paper book called a zigzag book. The front page of these books will show you the letters your child has learnt that week and the contents will only use the letters and words they have learnt so far. Listen to them say the sounds on the front page and then read the rest of the book to you. Ask them to tell you what the book was about and what happened. As they get further through the programme, the books become little stories. They will not bring home other reading books until this fifteen-week programme has been completed. From Week 3, a star word will also appear on the front of these zigzag books. Star words are words that cannot be built; they have to be learnt by sight.

From the end of Week 3, children will also bring home a minute track each week. These are lists of 30 words using the letters learnt so far. Children follow the track, reading the words as quickly as they can in order to reach the end of the track in one minute. Don't worry if they don't reach the end at the first attempt. Time them and, when one minute is up, stop them and tell them to colour in the word they have reached. Now they have a target to beat next time. Do it every day until they can reach the end of the track before one minute is up.

Praise, praise, praise your child's efforts. Show them how pleased you are with them and with what they are trying so hard to do. Even if they stumble, there is always something you can find to praise. Nothing succeeds like success – let them know that they are succeeding.

Alongside this programme, please continue to read to your child and provide the excitement that published books bring. Soon they will recognise some of the words on the page. This will show them the purpose of reading and that they, too, will be able to read these books before long.

With our combined efforts, by the end of this term, you will be surprised at how far your child has progressed along the road to reading.

Yours faithfully,

Teacher resources

Words list for Stage 1 – Weeks 1–6

Weeks 1 – 6: Short vowel and pure consonant sounds

Week 1: no star word   Week 2: no star word   Week 3 star word: I

a	t	n	s	i	d	l	r	e	p	m	f
a	at	an	as	if	dan	lad	ran	end	pad	am	fan
		ant	sat	in	din	lid	rat	den	pan	mad	fat
		tan	ants	is	sad	lit	rats	led	pant	man	fed
				it	dad	slid	rid	net	pat	map	felt
				sit	and	slit		ted	pats	mat	fin
				sits	sand			ten	pen	men	fit
				tins					pest	met	flip
									pet	mist	
									pip		
									plan		
									drip		
									lip		
									sip		
									tip		
									slip		
									spit		

Week 4 star word: my   Week 5 star word: the   Week 6 star word: to

o	c	g	h	u	b	v	w	j	k	y	z
on	can	gag	had	cup	bad	van	wag	jab	kid	yak	zap
nod	cap	gap	ham	fun	bag	vat	went	jam	kip	yap	zip
not	cat	get	hand	gum	ban	vet	west	jet	kit	yes	zigzag
pot	cod	got	hat	gun	band		wept	job	kept	yet	
spot	cop	cog	hem	hug	bat		wig	jolt	elk	yelp	
stop	cot	dog	hen	mug	beg		win	jug	milk	yum	
rod		fog	hid	mum	best		swept	junk	skid		
tom		log	him	nun	bet		swift	just	skin		
		peg	hip	pug	big				skip		
		pig	hit	pun	bin						
		glad	hog	sum	bit						
			hot	sun	bog						
					bud						
					bug						
					bun						
					but						
					bust						

Words List for Stage 2 – Weeks 7–9

Week 7 star word: of **Week 8 star word: was** **Week 9 star word: for**

ch	sh	th	tch	ck	ss	ll	ff	qu	ng	nk	x
chap	shed	than	batch	back	ass	shall	bluff	quack	bang	bank	tax
chat	shred	that	catch	pack	lass	bell	chaff	quick	fang	rank	wax
chest	shelf	them	hatch	rack	mass	dell	cliff	quid	gang	tank	flex
chin	shin	then	latch	sack	bless	fell	cuff	quins	hang	blank	next
chip	ship	this	match	shack	chess	sell	fluff	quit	rang	plank	vex
chimp	shift		patch	tack	dress	tell	gruff	quiz	sang	shrank	fix
chop	shop	with	snatch	black	less	shell	huff		clang	spank	mix
chug	shot	cloth	scratch	crack	mess	yell	off		slang	ink	six
chuff	shun	moth	fetch	smack	press	bill	puff		sprang	link	sixth
	shut	maths	sketch	snack	stress	fill	scuff		ding	mink	ox
bench		pith	stretch	track	hiss	hill	skiff		king	pink	box
bunch	ash	fifth	itch	deck	kiss	ill	sniff		ping	rink	fox
crunch	bash	sixth	ditch	neck	miss	kill	stiff		ring	sink	
drench	cash	smith	hitch	peck	boss	pill	stuff		sing	wink	
trench	dash	tenth	pitch	speck	cross	skill	tiff		wing	shrink	
finch	gash		witch	kick	loss	spill			bring	stink	
hunch	lash	thin	stitch	lick	moss	still			cling	think	
lunch	mash	thud	switch	pick	toss	will			fling	bunk	
munch	sash	thrift	hutch	sick	fuss	shrill			sling	junk	
much	clash	throb	clutch	thick		thrill			spring	drunk	
pinch	flash	thump	crutch	tick		doll			sting	trunk	
punch	slash	thrust		brick		dull			string		
rich	trash			click		skull			swing		
stitch	smash			prick					thing		
such	splash			stick					gong		
	mesh			dock					long		
	flesh			lock					song		
	fresh			rock					strong		
	dish			sock					bung		
	fish			block					dung		
	wish			clock					hung		
	swish			flock					lung		
				stock					rung		
	posh			shock					sung		
	hush			buck					clung		
	rush			duck					flung		
	mush			luck					sprung		
	blush			muck					stung		
	brush			suck							
	crush			cluck							
				pluck							
				truck							
				stuck							
				struck							

Words List for Stage 3 – Weeks 10–15

Week 10: Long vowels   Star word: he

a–e		i–e		o–e		u–e	
ape	hate	bite	pipe	bone	joke	brute	mule
bake	lake	dive	ride	code	nose	cube	plume
came	late	fine	ripe	coke	note	duke	prune
cape	made	hide	side	cone	robe	dune	rude
cave	pale	like	tide	dome	rode	flute	rule
date	same	line	time	doze	rope	june	tube
game	take	mile	wife	home	smoke	luke	tune
gate	wake	mine	wipe	hope	spoke		use
		nine					

Weeks 11–15: Vowel digraphs, vowels with r and other vowel forms

Week 11 star word: we   Week 12 star word: she   Week 13 star word: said

ee	ai	ay	oo	oa	oi/oy	ou	ow	ea	oo	aw	ow
bee	brain	bay	boot	boat	boil	bout	brown	bean	book	claw	blow
beef	chain	clay	broom	coat	coil	cloud	clown	beast	brook	dawn	bowl
cheek	fail	day	food	foal	coin	foul	cow	cheat	cook	draw	flow
cheep	hail	hay	gloom	goat	foil	mouth	crown	cream	foot	drawn	glow
deep	mail	jay	hoof	loaf	join	out	down	deal	good	hawk	show
feet	nail	may	hoop	moan	joint	pout	drown	heat	hook	jaw	throw
green	pail	pay	loop	roam	moist	scout	now	leaf	look	lawn	
keep	pain	ray	mood	soak	oil	shout	owl	lean	nook	paw	
meet	paint	say	moon	soap	point	south	town	meat	rook	raw	
peep	rail	play	noon	boast	soil	count		pea	took	saw	
see	rain	pray	shoot	coast	spoil	found		peach		yawn	
seed	sail	spray	spoon	stoat	toil	ground		peat			
sweet	snail	stay	roof	toast		hound		seat			
teeth	stain	stray	room			mound		scream			
three	tail	tray	root		boy	round		stream			
tree	train				joy			team			
week	wait				toy						

Week 14 star word: they   Week 15 star word: me

ar	ir	or	ur	er	ight	y	ew
bar	fir	for	fur	her	fight	by	chew
car	sir	cord	burn	fern	light	cry	drew
far	bird	cork	burst	herd	might	dry	few
tar	dirt	corn	church	kerb	night	fly	flew
bark	firm	ford	churn	perch	right	fry	grew
barn	girl	fork	curl	perm	sight	my	new
cart	kirk	form	furl	term	tight	shy	news
dark	shirt	fort	hurl	tern	bright	sly	newt
hark	skirt	pork	hurt		flight	sky	screw
harm	stir	port	surf		slight	spy	stew
harp		short	turf			sty	
park		stork	turn			try	
part		storm					
scarf							
shark							
sharp							

Letter fans

Cut out and use the letter fans to form words. Split pins can be used to hold fans together.

Letter fans

Cut out and use the letter fans to form words. Split pins can be used to hold fans together.

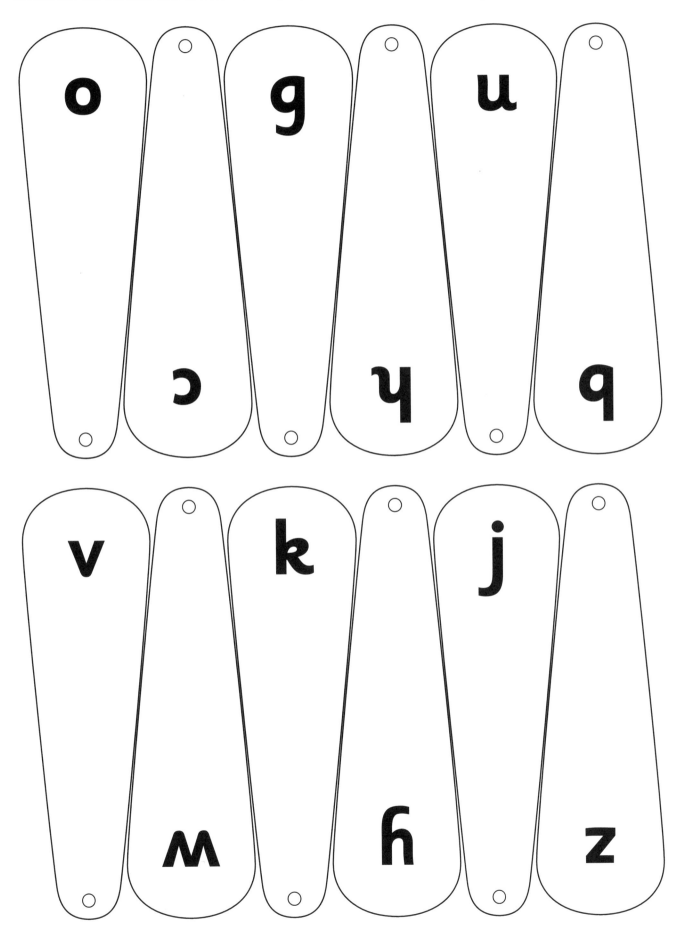

Letter fans

Cut out and use the letter fans to form words. Split pins can be used to hold fans together.

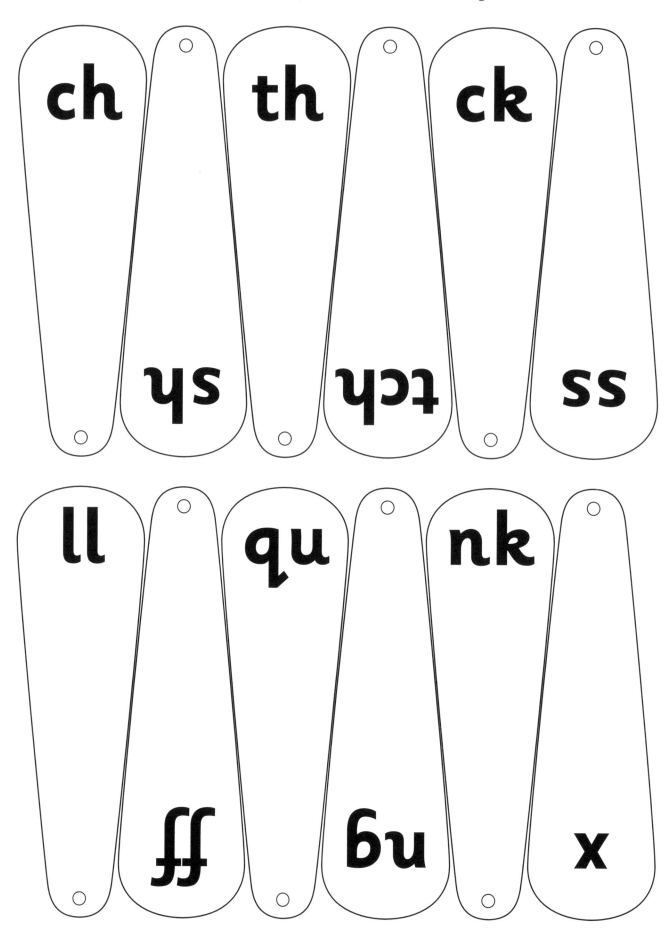

Letter fans

Cut out and use the letter fans to form words. Split pins can be used to hold fans together.

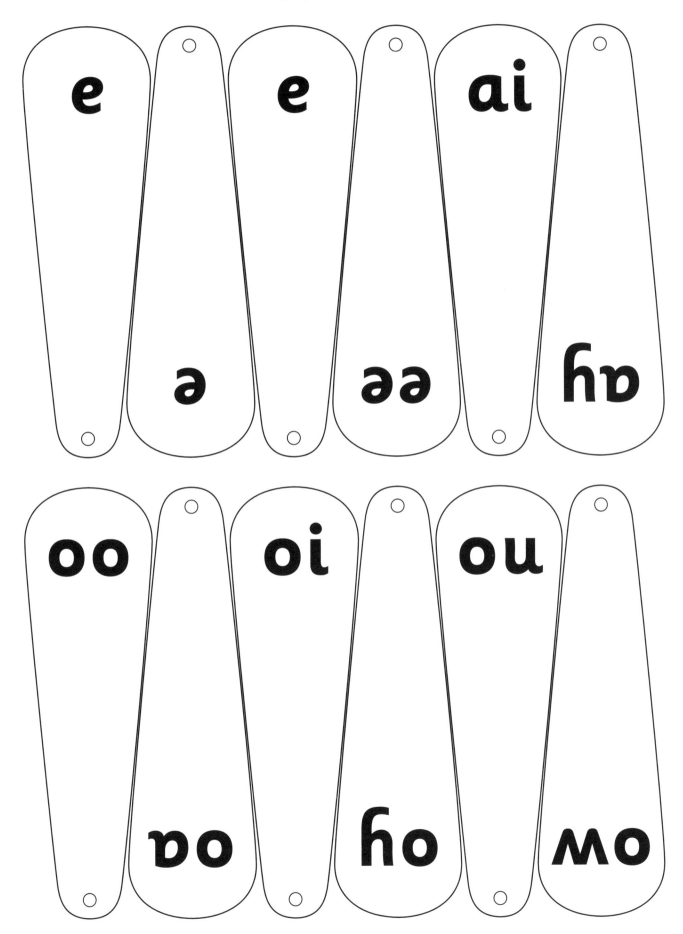

Letter fans

Cut out and use the letter fans to form words. Split pins can be used to hold fans together.

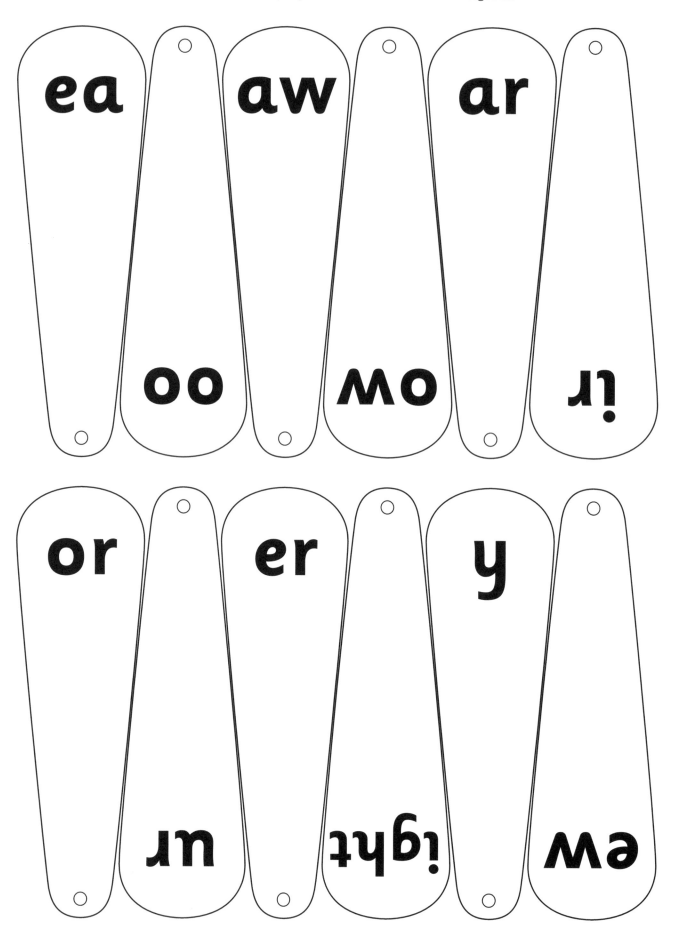

Letter sheets for word-building – Stage 1

Week 1	a	t	n	a
Week 2	i	d	l	r
Week 3	e	p	m	f

Classworks: The Synthetic Phonics Book © Helen Hadley, Nelson Thornes Ltd, 2006

Letter sheets for word-building – Stage 1

Week 4	o	c	g	h
Week 5	u	b	v	w
Week 6	k	y	j	z

Classworks: The Synthetic Phonics Book © Helen Hadley, Nelson Thornes Ltd. 2006

Letter sheets for word-building – Stage 2

Week 7	ch	sh	th	tch
Week 8	ck	ss	ll	ff
Week 9	qu	ng	nk	x

21

Classworks: The Synthetic Phonics Book © Helen Hadley, Nelson Thornes Ltd, 2006

Letter sheets for word-building – Stage 3

Week 10	e	e	e	e
Week 11	ee	ai	ay	oo
Week 12	oa	oi	ou	ow

Classworks: The Synthetic Phonics Book © Helen Hadley Nelson Thornes Ltd 2006

Letter sheets for word-building – Stage 3

Week 13	ea	oo	aw	ow
Week 14	ar	ir	or	ur
Week 15	er	y	igh	ew

Classworks: The Synthetic Phonics Book © Helen Hadley, Nelson Thornes Ltd, 2006

Star word outline

Copy and cut out the star. Write the star word of the week boldly and clearly in the middle.

Stage 1 – Weeks 1-6

**Week 1
Lesson plan**

Monday	a	Tuesday	t	Wednesday	n	Thursday	s

Follow this sequence for introducing these letters: **a, t, n, s**.

On the first day tell the children that they are going to start learning letters so they can learn to read. Follow this sequence for introducing a letter.

Identifying the sound

- Hold up items or pictures of items beginning with the day's letter.
- Ask the children what the items are.
- What sound can they hear at the beginning of each word?
- What can they tell you about these words? Yes, they all begin with the same sound. What sound is that?
- Say words beginning with the new sound; children say the word, then the sound it begins with.
- Is there anyone in the class whose name begins with this sound? Do they know anyone else whose name begins with the sound?
- Can they think of other words beginning with the day's sound?
- Say sentences with some words in them beginning with the day's sound, and ask them to tell you which words begin with that sound.
- Create a 'sound' table with a few items beginning with the letter. Children add things they find or bring from home beginning with the sound. Throughout the week add to the letter table, then send items home at the end of each week.
- From the first day – letter **a** – hang up the new letters. Use them in the daily ten-minute sessions.

Making the sound

Take time to practise the correct way to pronounce each sound before teaching it to the children, so you teach it correctly.

- /a/ is made at the back of the mouth with the mouth wide open.
- /t/, /n/, /s/ are made with the tongue behind slightly open teeth with the mouth slightly open.

Learning the sound

- Say it loudly, say it softly, say it rhythmically, say it slowly and then say it quickly several times.
- Hold up or point to pictures of things beginning with the day's letter, e.g. 'ant'. Emphasise the /a/ and /n/ but not the /t/ – e.g. aaannt – 'ant' etc. Keep the /t/ sound short, a pure sound not /tuh/ or /ter/. Say the word slowly at first then gradually get up to normal speed.
- Use the large, laminated letters (from the ten-minute sessions) and hold up the one with today's letter on it, saying, "This is today's letter. It is ... What does it say? Yes, it says ..."
- Put it with a few other letters and show them to the children. Ask them to put their hands up as soon as they see today's letter.
- Write words using known letters and ask, "What does this word say?"
- Do not use sentences in Week 1.

25

Writing the new letter

Do this section with the children sitting at their tables with crayons, pencils and paper in front of them.

- Draw the day's letter on the board as large as you can, saying the letter as you write it.
- Facing the children, tell them to stand up.
- Say the letter slowly as you draw a huge mirror image of its shape right across your body with a pointing finger. Now ask the children to do it with you. For example, you point to your left to start the shape for the letter **a** and say "Start this side," the children will point to their right. By facing the children you can see whether they are starting in the right place and shaping the letter correctly. Stretch up, bend, reaching from side to side, using all your body space to make the letter really huge.
- Do this several times together and separately. Check that they are forming the shape correctly.
- Ask them to sit down and draw the letter's shape with their finger on the table top saying its sound at the same time.
- Let them cover the paper with the letter, writing it in pencil and with crayons of different colours, writing it big, writing it small.
- Walk round and check that the children are using a triangular pencil grip, and correct as necessary.

Worksheet activities

Children use the worksheet for the day's letter to reinforce how to:

1 form the letter – go over it with a finger then several times with both pencil and crayons; (Draw a replica of the shape on the board and show children how to follow the arrows to complete the word.)
2 write the letter – trace over the printed letters, then write it between the lines;
3 find the letter – circle the correct one for each picture.

If you have a classroom assistant or helper they should repeat the session later in the day for reinforcement with slow learners (or those who have been absent).

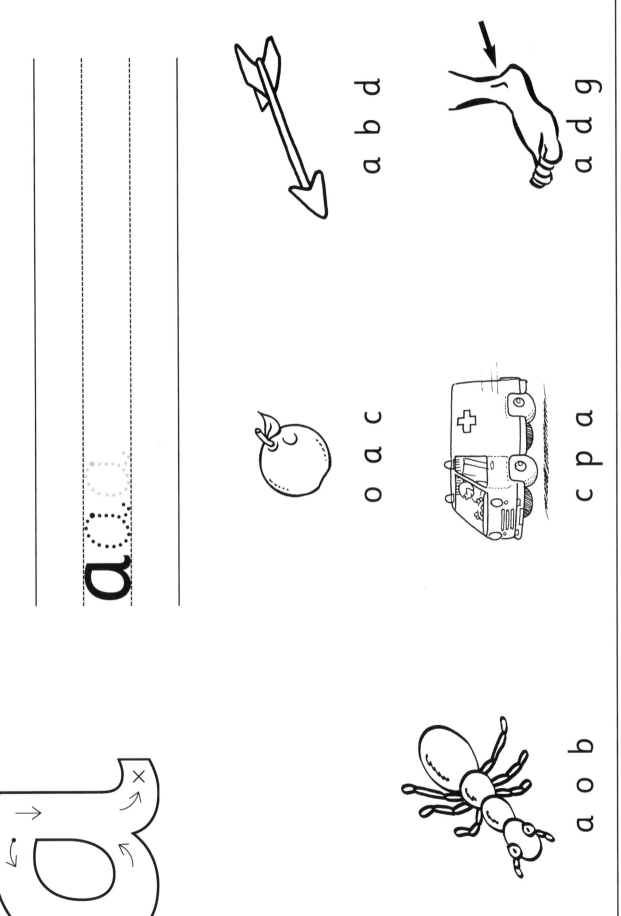

a b d

a d g

o a c

c p a

a o b

1. Follow arrows to write large letter.   2. Go over letter on lines then write it.   3. Circle correct letter for each picture.

Classworks: The Synthetic Phonics Book © Helen Hadley, Nelson Thornes Ltd, 2006

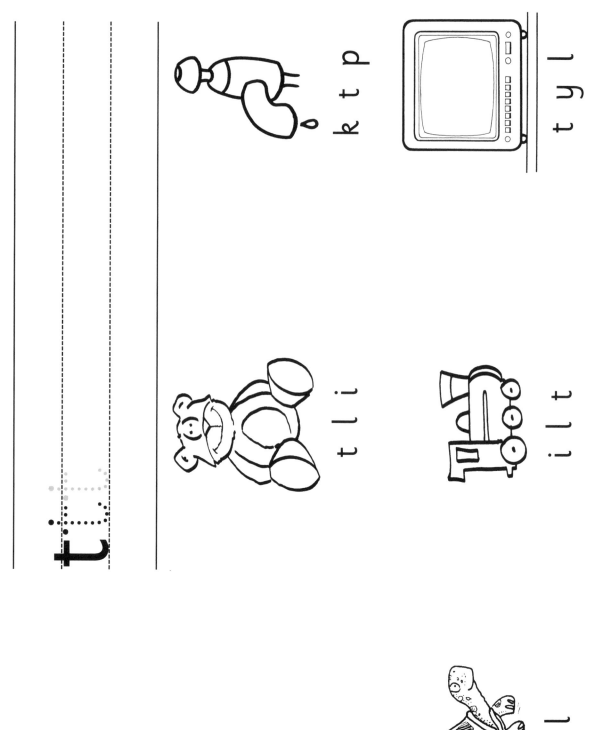

k t p

t y l

t l i

i l t

f t l

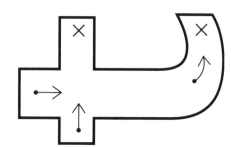

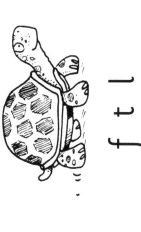

1. Follow arrows to write large letter.   2. Go over letter on lines then write it.   3. Circle correct letter for each picture.

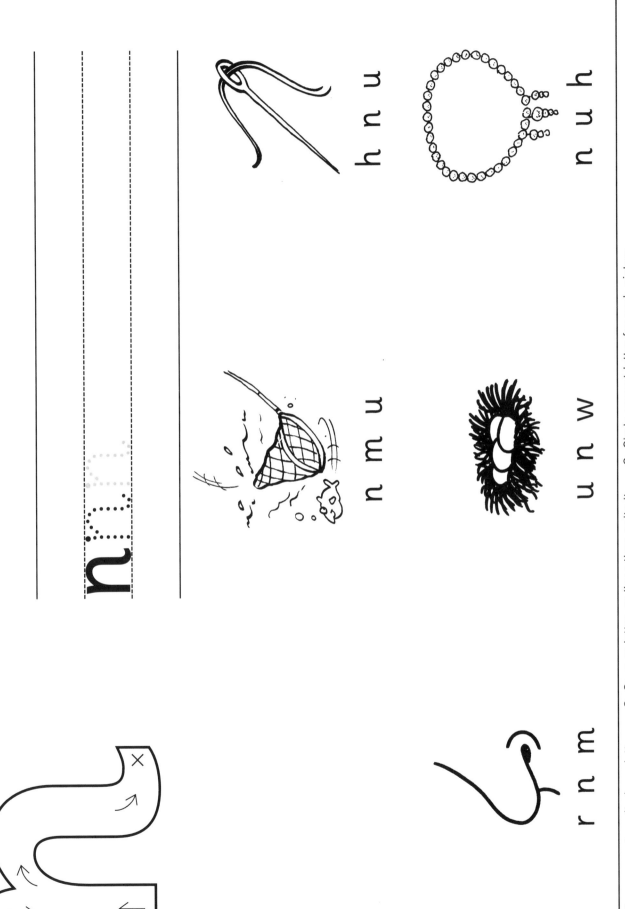

h n u

n u h

n m u

u n w

r n m

1. Follow arrows to write large letter.   2. Go over letter on lines then write it.   3. Circle correct letter for each picture.

Classworks: The Synthetic Phonics Book © Helen Hadley, Nelson Thornes Ltd, 2006

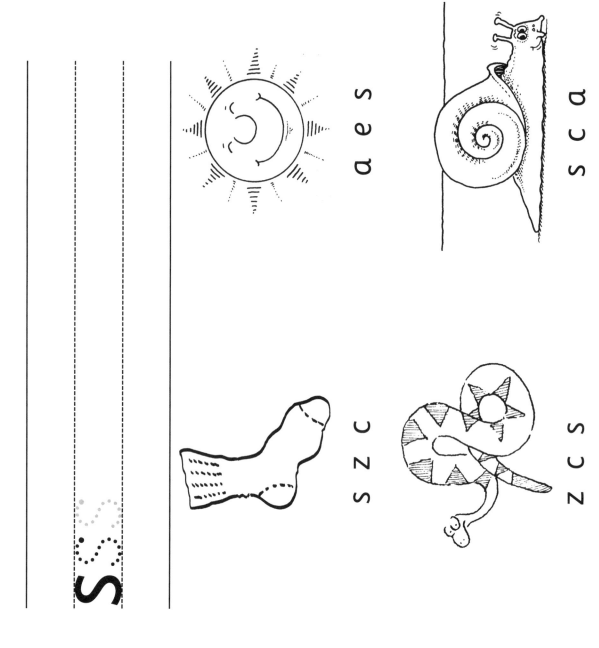

a   e   s

s   c   a

s   z   c

z   c   s

s   k   c

1. Follow arrows to write large letter.   2. Go over letter on lines then write it.   3. Circle correct letter for each picture.

30

Week 1
Friday review

Preparation

- Have ready the laminated cards of letters learnt to date.

Revision

- Holding up each of this week's letters in turn, you say, "This is **a**. What is it?" The children say the sound of the letter.
- Go through the letters for the children to respond to, getting faster and faster.
- Give out three copies of this week's letters, and have a copy of each for yourself. For the first three weeks, children share with their neighbours so they help each other with letter recognition.
- Holding up one of this week's letters ask, "What is this letter?" They respond. "If you have letter **a**, hold it up." Do this for all of this week's letters several times. Remember not to use the letter names.
- Say one of this week's letters and invite someone to come and write that letter on the board. Do this for all of this week's letters several times.
- Using the word list, ask the children to come out if they have any of the letters for a word you give them, e.g. hold up the letters for the word 'an'. "What does this word say? Come out if you have any of the letters for the word 'an'." Children sharing a letter take turns to come out with their letter.
- Using the word list for reference, say a word and ask the children to come out if they have any of the letters from that word.
- Use the letter fans for this week's letters for word-building activities – see games and activities, page 5.
- The word lists can also be used to check the progress of individual children.
- Each week, select a few children to check their progress on the minute tracks and to hear them read the zigzag book. You may need to check on some children more frequently than others to ensure they keep up.

This week's word list

a

an

at

as

ant

ants

31

Matching sounds and pictures

1. Say the letter sounds.   2. Say what is in each picture.   3. Draw a line to join the correct letter to its picture.

5

as
s
a

4

a
t
at

6

as
at
an
a

3

a
n
an

7

an ant

2

a
n
t
s

8

ants

1

Week 1
letters: a n t s

Fold across the middle and make a zigzag book.   Sound the letters then read the book.

33

**Week 2
Lesson plan**

Monday	**i**	Tuesday	**d**	Wednesday	**l**	Thursday	**r**

Follow this sequence for introducing these letters: **i**, **d**, **l**, **r**.

Remind children that the more letters they learn, the more words they can read.

Identifying the sound

- Hold up items or pictures of items beginning with the day's letter.
- Ask the children what the items are.
- What sound can they hear at the beginning of each word?
- What can they tell you about these words? Yes, they all begin with the same sound. What sound is that?
- Say words beginning with the new sound; children say the word, then the sound it begins with.
- Is there anyone in the class whose name begins with this sound? Do they know anyone else whose name begins with the sound?
- Can they think of other words beginning with the day's sound?
- Say sentences with some words in them beginning with the day's sound, and ask them to tell you which words begin with that sound.
- Create a 'sound' table with a few items beginning with the letter. Children add things they find or bring from home beginning with the sound. Throughout the week add to the letter table, then send items home at the end of each week.
- Hang up the new letters. Use them in daily ten-minute sessions.

Making the sound

Take time to practise the correct way to pronounce each sound with the children.

- /i/ is a hard sound at the back of the mouth said with a smiling mouth.
- /d/, /l/, /r/ are made with the tongue behind slightly open teeth with the mouth slightly open.

Learning the sound

- Say it loudly, say it softly, say it rhythmically, say it slowly and then say it quickly several times.
- Hold up or point to pictures of things beginning with the day's letter. Emphasise the vowel, e.g. diiin – 'din' etc. Keep the /d/, /l/ and /r/ sounds short, pure sounds not /duh/ or /der/, /luh/ or /ler/, /ruh/ or /rer/.
- Use the large, laminated letters (from the ten-minute sessions) and hold up the one with today's letter on it, saying, "This is today's letter. It is … What does it say? Yes, it says …"
- Put it with a few other letters and show them to the children. Ask them to put their hands up as soon as they see today's letter.
- Write words using known letters and ask, "What does this word say?"
- Start to use short sentences, e.g. "It is an ant."

Writing the new letter

Do this section with the children sitting at their tables with crayons, pencils and paper in front of them.

- Draw the day's letter on the board as large as you can, saying the letter as you write it.

- Facing the children, tell them to stand up.
- Say the letter slowly as you draw a huge mirror image of its shape right across your body with a pointing finger. Now ask the children to do it with you. By facing the children you can see whether they are starting in the right place and shaping the letter correctly. Stretch up, bend, reaching from side to side, use all your body space to make the letter really huge.
- Do this several times together and separately. Check that they are forming the shape correctly.
- Ask them to sit down and draw the letter's shape with their finger on the table top saying its sound at the same time.
- Let them cover the paper with the letter, writing it in pencil and with crayons of different colours, writing it big, writing it small.
- Walk round and check that the children are using a triangular pencil grip, and correct as necessary.

Worksheet activities

Children use the worksheet for the day's letter to reinforce how to:

1 form the letter – go over it with a finger then several times with both pencil and crayons; (Draw a replica of the shape on the board and show children how to follow the arrows to complete the word.)
2 write the letter – trace over the printed letters, then write it between the lines;
3 find the letter – circle the correct one for each picture.

If you have a classroom assistant or helper they should repeat the session later in the day for reinforcement with slow learners (or those who have been absent).

Classworks Synthetic Phonics Photocopiable Readers

The following Photocopiable Readers can be used this week:

- a rat and an ant
- dan and a lid.

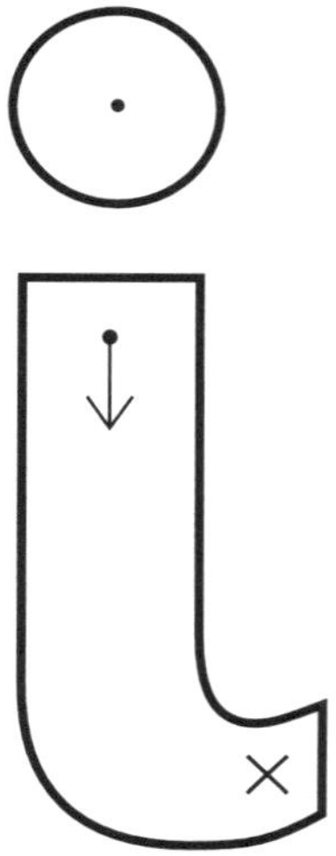

j l i

t s i

i f t

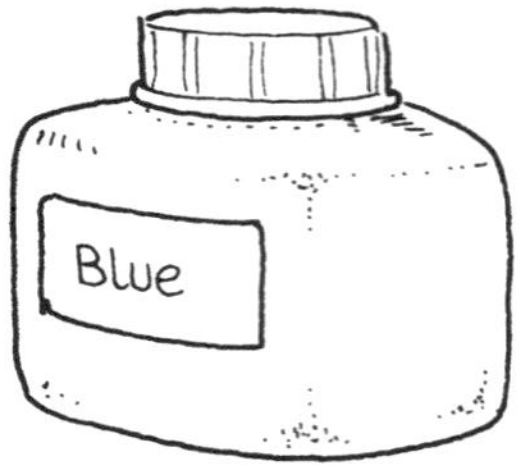

a i t

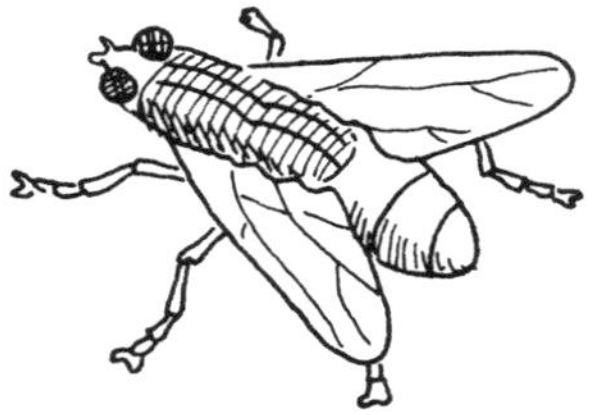

Blue

i t n

1. Follow arrows to write large letter. 2. Go over letter on lines then write it. 3. Circle correct letter for each picture.

Classworks: The Synthetic Phonics Book © Helen Hadley, Nelson Thornes Ltd, 2006

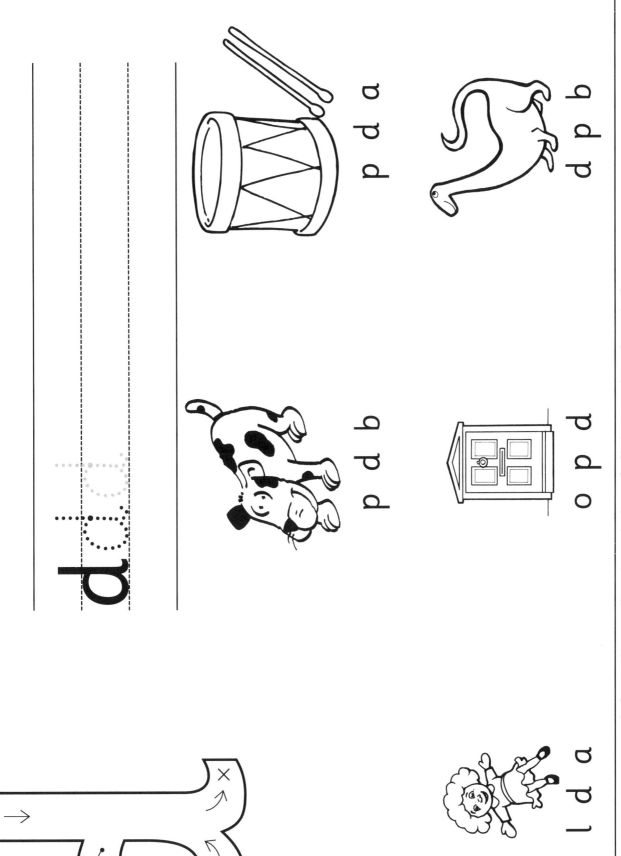

p d a

d p b

p d b

o p d

l d a

1. Follow arrows to write large letter.   2. Go over letter on lines then write it.   3. Circle correct letter for each picture.

Classworks: The Synthetic Phonics Book © Helen Hadley, Nelson Thornes Ltd, 2006

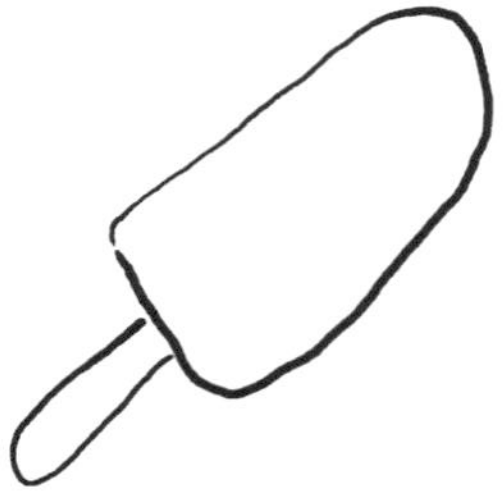

STAGE 1 | WEEK 2 | WORKSHEET 3

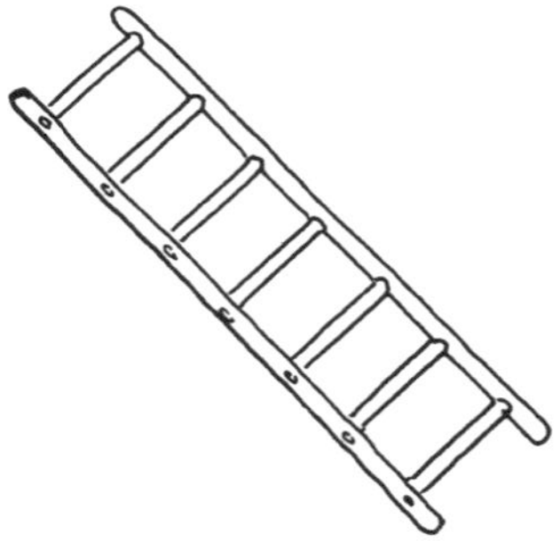

l t i

j t l

t l k

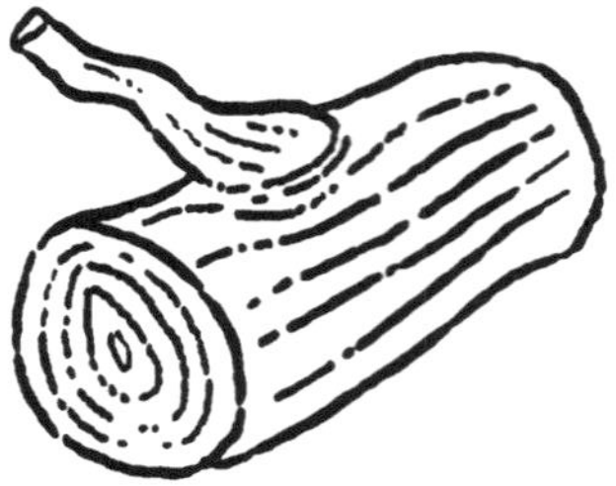

l i t

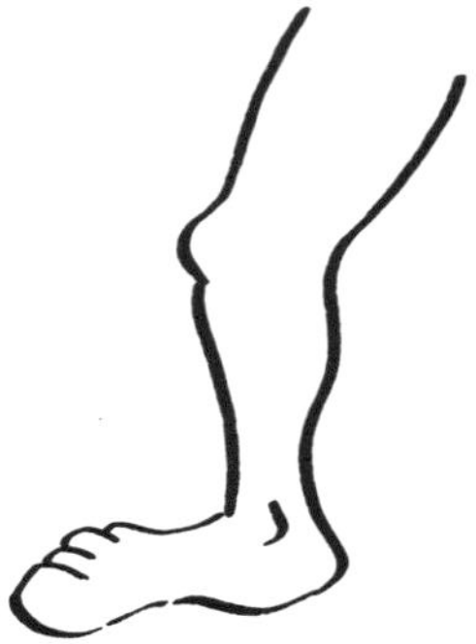

j i l

1. Follow arrows to write large letter.   2. Go over letter on lines then write it.   3. Circle correct letter for each picture.

Classworks: The Synthetic Phonics Book © Helen Hadley Nelson Thornes Ltd 2006

38

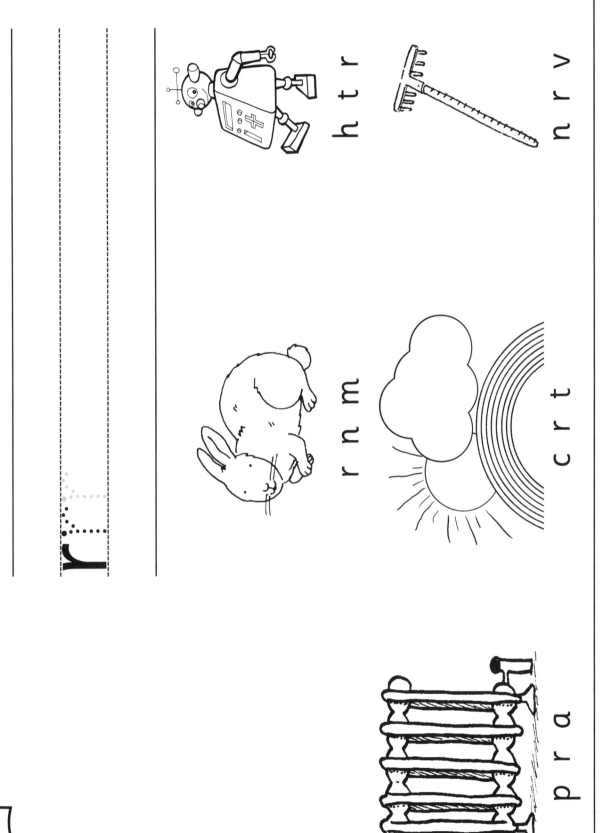

h t r

n r v

r n m

c r t

p r a

r

1. Follow arrows to write large letter.   2. Go over letter on lines then write it.   3. Circle correct letter for each picture.

Classworks: The Synthetic Phonics Book © Helen Hadley, Nelson Thornes Ltd, 2006

Week 2
Friday review

Preparation

- Have ready the laminated cards of letters learnt to date.

Revision

- Holding up each of this week's letters in turn, you say, "This is **i**. What is it?" The children say the sound of the letter.
- Go through the letters for the children to respond to, getting faster and faster.
- Give out three copies of letters learnt to date, and have a copy of each yourself. For the first three weeks, children share with their neighbours so they help each other with letter recognition.
- Holding up one of this week's letters ask, "What is this letter?" They respond. "If you have letter **i**, hold it up." Do this for all of this week's letters several times.
- Say one of this week's letters and invite someone to come and write that letter on the board. Do this for all of this week's letters several times.
- Using the word list, ask the children to come out if they have any of the letters for a word you give them, e.g. hold up the letters for the word 'it'. "What does this word say? Come out if you have any of the letters for the word 'it'." Children sharing a letter take turns to come out with their letter.
- Using the word list for reference, say a word and ask the children to come out if they have any of the letters from that word.
- Use the letter fans for this week's letters for word-building activities – see games and activities, page 5.
- The word lists can also be used to check the progress of individual children.
- Each week, select a few children to check their progress on the minute tracks and to hear them read the zigzag book. You may need to check on some children more frequently than others to ensure they keep up.

This week's word list

it	lid
tin	rats
sad	and
ran	sand
did	land

Matching sounds and pictures

1. Say the letter sounds.   2. Say what is in each picture.   3. Draw a line to join the correct letter to its picture.

Classworks: The Synthetic Phonics Book © Helen Hadley, Nelson Thornes Ltd, 2006

a lid

4

an ant

3

ant
lid
rat
tin

2

Week 2
letters: i d l r

1

an ant in a
lid

5

a rat

6

a tin

7

a rat in a tin

8

Fold across the middle and make a zigzag book.   Sound the letters then read the book.

Classworks: The Synthetic Phonics Book © Helen Hadley, Nelson Thornes Ltd 2006

42

**Week 3
Lesson plan**

| Monday | *e* | Tuesday | **p** | Wednesday | m | Thursday | *f* |

Follow this sequence for introducing these letters: *e*, **p**, **m**, *f*.

Remind children that the more letters they learn, the more words they can read.

Identifying the sound

- Hold up items or pictures of items beginning with the day's letter.
- Ask the children what the items are.
- What sound can they hear at the beginning of each word?
- What can they tell you about these words? Yes, they all begin with the same sound. What sound is that?
- Say words beginning with the new sound; children say the word, then the sound it begins with.
- Is there anyone in the class whose name begins with this sound? Do they know anyone else whose name begins with the sound?
- Can they think of other words beginning with the day's sound?
- Say sentences with some words in them beginning with the day's sound, and ask them to tell you which words begin with that sound.
- Create a 'sound' table with a few items beginning with the letter. Children add things they find or bring from home beginning with the sound. Throughout the week add to the letter table, then send items home at the end of each week.
- Hang up the new letters. Use them in daily ten-minute sessions.

Making the sound

Take time to practise the correct way to pronounce each sound with the children.

- /e/ is a hard sound made at the back of the mouth with a smiling mouth.
- /p/ is a slight popping sound as air is forced out of closed lips.
- /m/ is made by pressing the lips together and making a humming sound.
- /f/ is made by biting the bottom lip and pushing air out of the mouth.

Learning the sound

- Say it loudly, say it softly, say it rhythmically, say it slowly and then say it quickly several times.
- Hold up or point to pictures of things beginning with the day's letter. Emphasise the vowel, e.g. faaan – 'fan' etc. Keep the /p/, /m/ and /f/ sounds short, pure sounds not /puh/ or /per/, /muh/ or /mer/, /fuh/ or /fer/.
- Use the large, laminated letters (from the ten-minute sessions) and hold up the one with today's letter on it, saying, "This is today's letter. It is … What does it say? Yes, it says …"
- Put it with a few other letters and show them to the children. Ask them to put their hands up as soon as they see today's letter.
- Write words using known letters and ask, "What does this word say?"
- Use short sentences containing this week's letters.

Writing the new letter

Do this section with the children sitting at their tables with crayons, pencils and paper in front of them.

43

- Draw the day's letter on the board as large as you can, saying the letter as you write it.
- Facing the children, tell them to stand up.
- Say the letter slowly as you draw a huge mirror image of its shape right across your body with a pointing finger. Now ask the children to do it with you. By facing the children you can see whether they are starting in the right place and shaping the letter correctly. Stretch up, bend, reaching from side to side, use all your body space to make the letter really huge.
- Do this several times together and separately. Check that they are forming the shape correctly.
- Ask them to sit down and draw the letter's shape with their finger on the table top saying its sound at the same time.
- Let them cover the paper with the letter, writing it in pencil and with crayons of different colours, writing it big, writing it small.
- Walk round and check that the children are using a triangular pencil grip, and correct as necessary.

Worksheet activities

Children use the worksheet for the day's letter to reinforce how to:

1 form the letter – go over it with a finger then several times with both pencil and crayons. (Draw a replica of the shape on the board and show children how to follow the arrows to complete the word.)
2 write the letter – trace over the printed letters, then write it between the lines.
3 find the letter – circle the correct one for each picture.

If you have a classroom assistant or helper they should repeat the session later in the day for reinforcement with slow learners (or those who have been absent).

Star word:

- Hold up the star word and ask if anyone knows the word.
- Say the word and ask the children to repeat it.
- Ask them why star words are different. Remind them that they are tricky words; words they have to know by looking at them, not by trying to build them.
- Say sentences with the word 'I' in them. Ask them to make up some for you.
- Hang up the star word and refer back to it at times during each day when you or they use the word, so they hear it in common usage.

Classworks Synthetic Phonics Photocopiable Readers

The following Photocopiable Readers can be used this week:

- dad's pet
- ned's tent
- sam, pip and the rats
- sad fred.

I

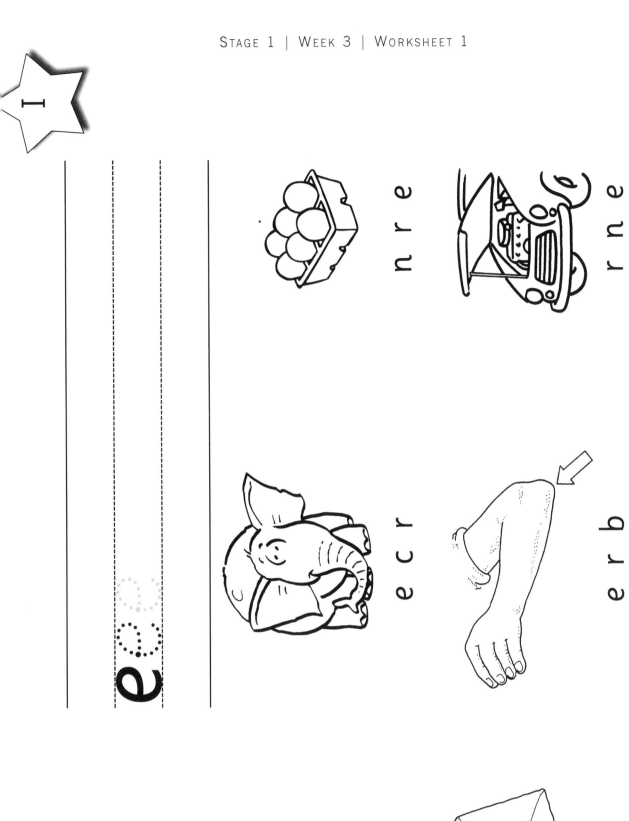

n r e

n r e

e c r

e r b

n c e

1. Follow arrows to write large letter.   2. Go over letter on lines then write it.   3. Circle correct letter for each picture.

Classworks: The Synthetic Phonics Book © Helen Hadley, Nelson Thornes Ltd, 2006

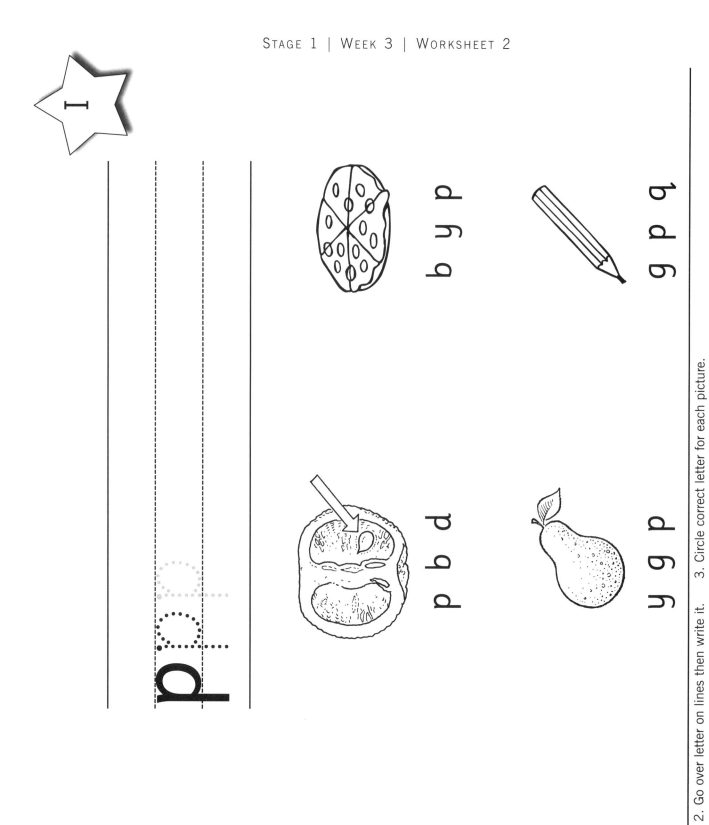

b y p

p b d

g d b

h g d

b d

d p b

1. Follow arrows to write large letter.   2. Go over letter on lines then write it.   3. Circle correct letter for each picture.

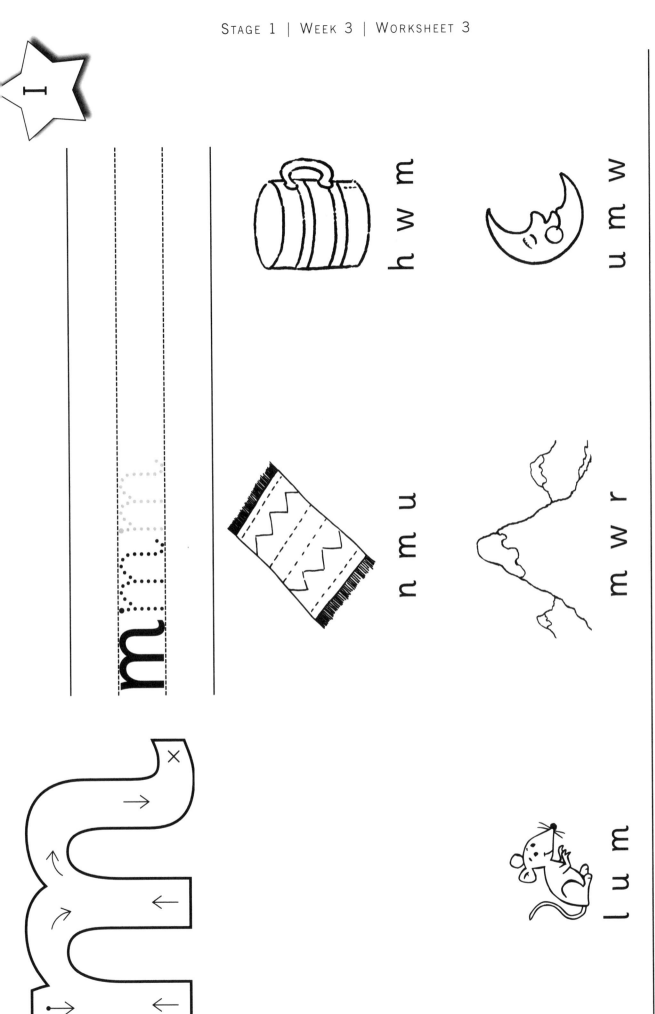

m

h w m

u m w

n m u

m w r

l u m

1. Follow arrows to write large letter.   2. Go over letter on lines then write it.   3. Circle correct letter for each picture.

Classworks: The Synthetic Phonics Book © Helen Hadley, Nelson Thornes Ltd, 2006

47

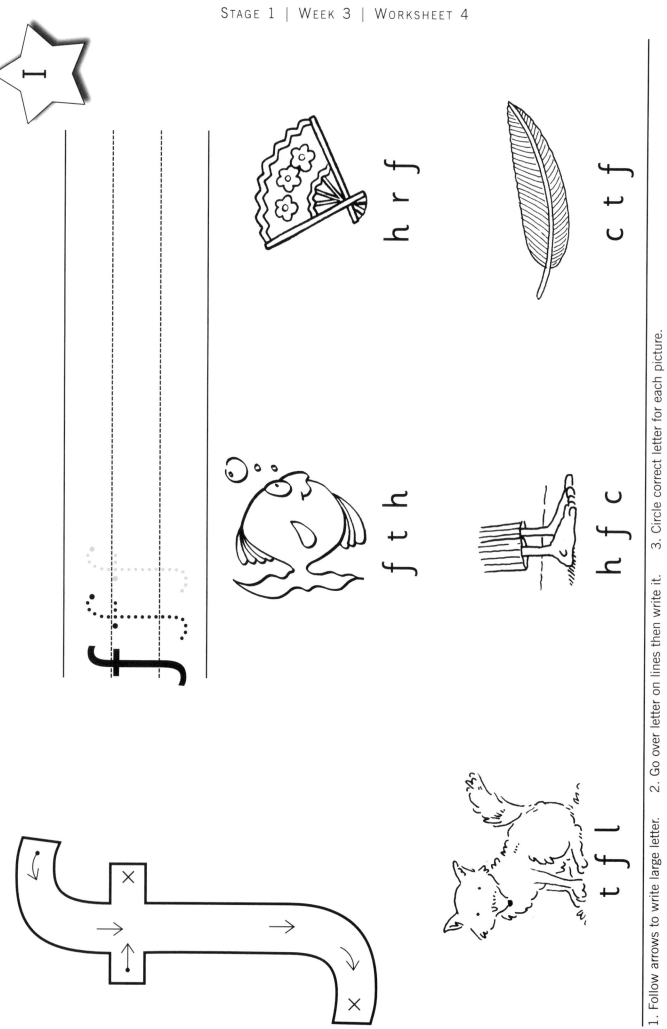

I

f

h r f

c t f

f t h

h f c

t f l

1. Follow arrows to write large letter.   2. Go over letter on lines then write it.   3. Circle correct letter for each picture.

Classworks: The Synthetic Phonics Book © Helen Hadley Nelson Thornes Ltd 2006

Week 3
Friday review

Preparation

- Have ready the laminated cards of letters learnt to date.

Revision

- Holding up each of this week's letters in turn, you say, "This is **e**. What is it?" The children say the sound of the letter.
- Go through the letters for the children to respond to, getting faster and faster.
- Give out three copies of letters learnt to date, and have a copy of each yourself. For the first three weeks, children share with their neighbours so they help each other with letter recognition.
- Holding up one of this week's letters ask, "What is this letter?" They respond. "If you have letter **e**, hold it up." Do this for all of this week's letters several times.
- Say one of this week's letters and invite someone to come and write that letter on the board. Do this for all of this week's letters several times.
- Using the word list, ask the children to come out if they have any of the letters for a word you give them, e.g. hold up the letters for the word 'pet'. "What does this word say? Come out if you have any of the letters for the word 'pet'." Children sharing a letter take turns to come out with their letter.
- Using the word list for reference, say a word and ask the children to come out if they have any of the letters from that word.
- Use the letter fans for this week's letters for word-building activities – see games and activities, page 5.
- The word lists can also be used to check the progress of individual children.
- Each week, select a few children to check their progress on the minute tracks and to hear them read the zigzag book. You may need to check on some children more frequently than others to ensure they keep up.

This week's word list

pet   lip

mat   fin

net   nest

fat   stamp

tap

pen

Matching sounds and pictures

1. Say the letter sounds.　　2. Say what is in each picture.　　3. Draw a line to join the correct letter to its picture.

Run the Track

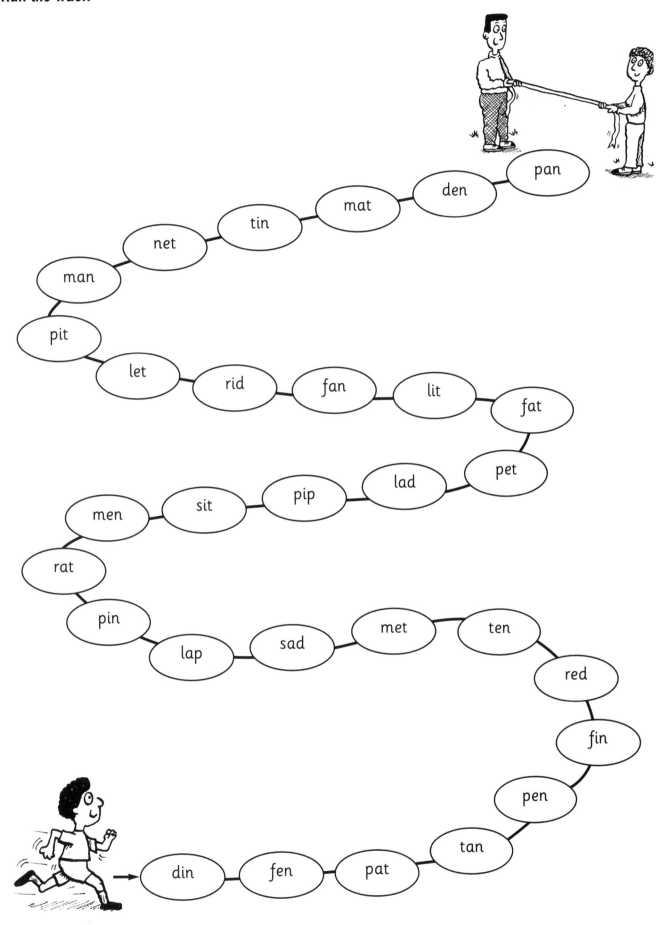

Can you reach the tape in 1 minute?

in it is a red mat	ted and I met in ted's den
5	4
ted and I sit on a red mat	I am ted's pet
6	3
an ant is in ted's den	I am fat sam
7	2
ted felt it nip him	Week 3 letters: e p m f
8	1

Fold across the middle and make a zigzag book.   Sound the letters then read the book.

Classworks: The Synthetic Phonics Book © Helen Hadley Nelson Thornes Ltd 2006

52

Week 4
Lesson plan

| Monday | **o** | Tuesday | **c** | Wednesday | **g** | Thursday | **h** |

Follow this sequence for introducing these letters: **o**, **c**, **g**, **h**.

Remind children that the more letters they learn, the more words they can read.

Identifying the sound

- Hold up items or pictures of items beginning with the day's letter.
- Ask the children what the items are.
- What sound can they hear at the beginning of each word?
- What can they tell you about these words? Yes, they all begin with the same sound. What sound is that?
- Say words beginning with the new sound; children say the word, then the sound it begins with.
- Is there anyone in the class whose name begins with this sound? Do they know anyone else whose name begins with the sound?
- Can they think of other words beginning with the day's sound?
- Say sentences with some words in them beginning with the day's sound, and ask them to tell you which words begin with that sound.
- Create a 'sound' table with a few items beginning with the letter. Children add things they find or bring from home beginning with the sound. Throughout the week add to the letter table, then send items home at the end of each week.
- Hang up the new letters. Use them in daily ten-minute sessions.

Making the sound

Take time to practise the correct way to pronounce each sound with the children.

- /o/ is made by pushing the lips forward making the mouth into an o shape then make a hard sound at the back of the mouth.
- /c/, /g/, /h/ – put your hand under the chin back against your throat and make a clicking sound at the back of the throat.

Learning the sound

- Say it loudly, say it softly, say it rhythmically, say it slowly and then say it quickly several times.
- Hold up or point to pictures of things beginning with the day's letter. Emphasise the vowel, e.g. caaan – 'can' etc. Keep the /c/, /g/ and /h/ sounds short, pure sounds not /cuh/ or /cer/, /guh/ or /ger/, /huh/ or /her/.
- Use the large, laminated letters (from the ten-minute sessions) and hold up the one with today's letter on it, saying, "This is today's letter. It is … What does it say? Yes, it says …"
- Put it with a few other letters and show them to the children. Ask them to put their hands up as soon as they see today's letter.
- Write words using known letters and ask, "What does this word say?"
- Use short sentences containing this week's letters.

Writing the new letter

Do this section with the children sitting at their tables with crayons, pencils and paper in front of them.

- Draw the day's letter on the board as large as you can, saying the letter as you write it.
- Facing the children, tell them to stand up.
- Say the letter slowly as you draw a huge mirror image of its shape right across your body with a pointing finger. Now ask the children to do it with you. By facing the children you can see whether they are starting in the right place and shaping the letter correctly. Stretch up, bend, reaching from side to side, use all your body space to make the letter really huge.
- Do this several times together and separately. Check that they are forming the shape correctly.
- Ask them to sit down and draw the letter's shape with their finger on the table top saying its sound at the same time.
- Let them cover the paper with the letter, writing it in pencil and with crayons of different colours, writing it big, writing it small.
- Walk round and check that the children are using a triangular pencil grip, and correct as necessary.

Worksheet activities

Children use the worksheet for the day's letter to reinforce how to:

1 form the letter – go over it with a finger then several times with both pencil and crayons; (Draw a replica of the shape on the board and show children how to follow the arrows to complete the word.)
2 write the letter – trace over the printed letters, then write it between the lines;
3 find the letter – circle the correct letter for the top line of pictures;
4 write the words for the bottom line of pictures.

If you have a classroom assistant or helper they should repeat the session later in the day for reinforcement with slow learners (or those who have been absent).

Star word:

- Hold up the star word and ask if anyone knows the word.
- Say the word and ask the children to repeat it.
- Ask them why star words are different. Remind them that they are tricky words; words they have to know by looking at them, not by trying to build them.
- Say sentences with the word 'my' in them. Ask them to make up some for you.
- Hang up the star word and refer back to it at times during each day when you or they use the word, so they hear it in common usage.

Classworks Synthetic Phonics Photocopiable Readers

The following Photocopiable Readers can be used this week:

- lots of pets
- I sit
- tom and greg
- my pets.

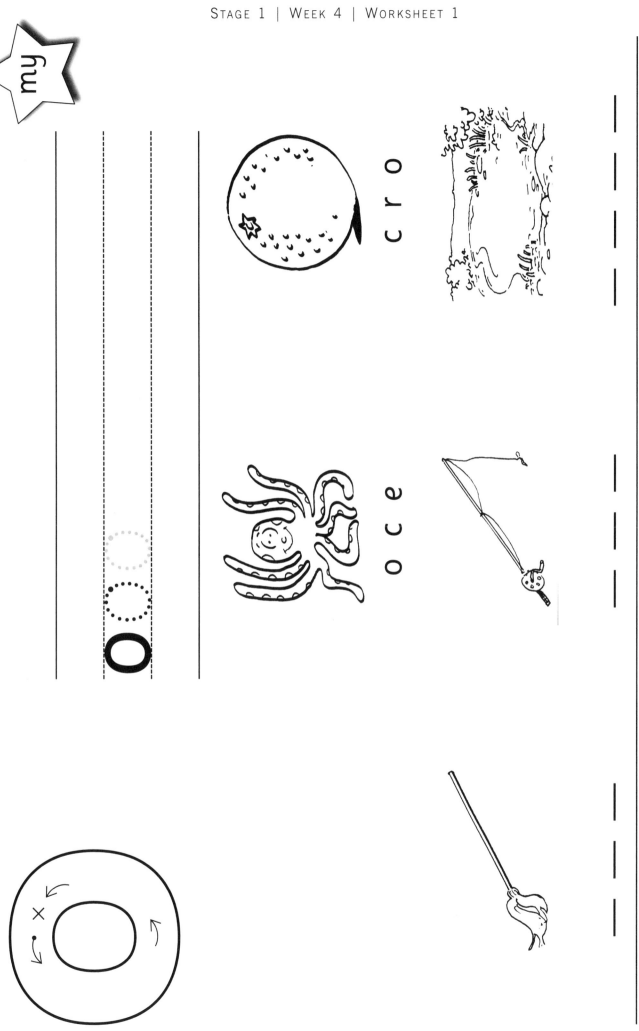

my

c r o

o c e

1. Follow arrows to write large letter.   2. Go over letter on lines then write it.   3. Circle correct letter for top line of pictures.   4. Write words for bottom line of pictures

Classworks: The Synthetic Phonics Book © Helen Hadley, Nelson Thornes Ltd, 2006

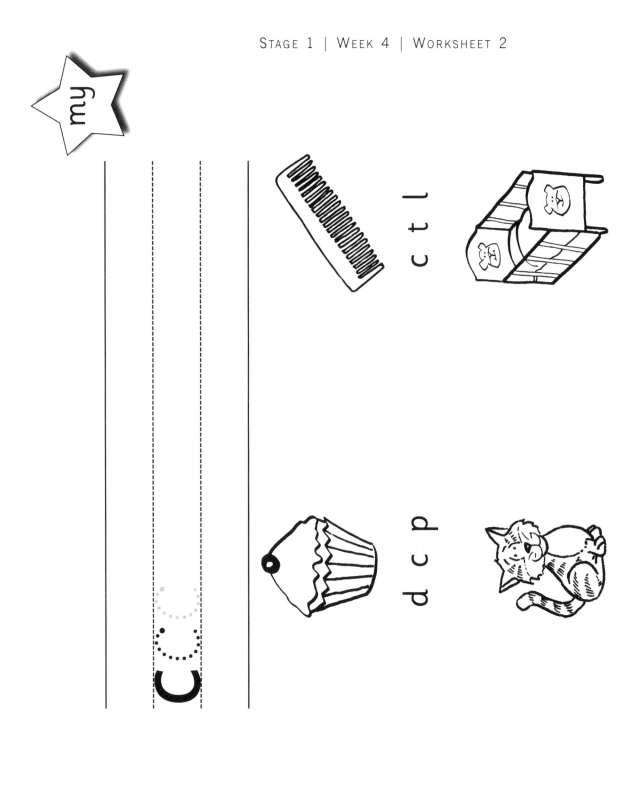

my

C

c t l

d c p

1. Follow arrows to write large letter.   2. Go over letter on lines then write it.   3. Circle correct letter for top line of pictures.   4. Write words for bottom line of pictures

56

my

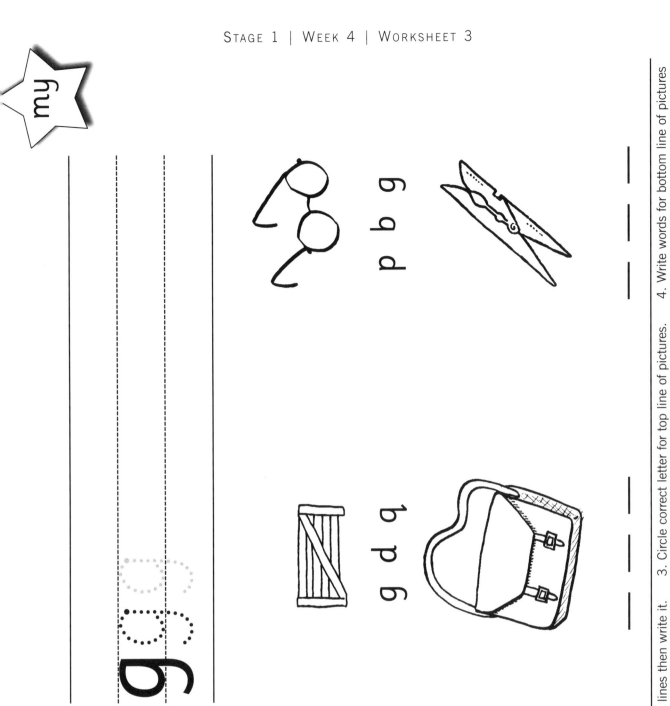

g

g

b q d

g p b

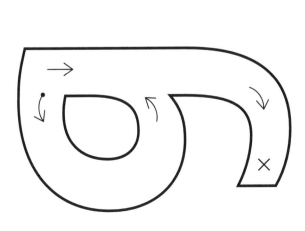

1. Follow arrows to write large letter.   2. Go over letter on lines then write it.   3. Circle correct letter for top line of pictures.   4. Write words for bottom line of pictures.

Classworks: The Synthetic Phonics Book © Helen Hadley, Nelson Thornes Ltd, 2006

my

h

h

c h a

n r h

58

1. Follow arrows to write large letter.   2. Go over letter on lines then write it.   3. Circle correct letter for top line of pictures.   4. Write words for bottom line of pictures

Classworks: The Synthetic Phonics Book © Helen Hadley, Nelson Thornes Ltd, 2006

Week 4
Friday review

Preparation

- Have ready the laminated cards of letters learnt to date.

Revision

- Holding up each of this week's letters in turn, you say, "This is **o**. What is it?" The children say the sound of the letter.
- Go through the letters for the children to respond to, getting faster and faster.
- Give out three copies of letters learnt to date, and have a copy of each yourself.
- Holding up one of this week's letters ask, "What is this letter?" They respond. "If you have letter **o**, hold it up." Do this for all of this week's letters several times.
- Say one of this week's letters and invite someone to come and write that letter on the board. Do this for all of this week's letters several times.
- Using the word list, ask the children to come out if they have any of the letters for a word you give them, e.g. hold up the letters for the word 'on'. "What does this word say? Come out if you have any of the letters for the word 'on'."
- Using the word list for reference, say a word and ask the children to come out if they have any of the letters from that word.
- Use the letter fans for this week's letters for word-building activities – see games and activities, page 5.
- The word lists can also be used to check the progress of individual children.
- Each week, select a few children to check their progress on the minute tracks and to hear them read the zigzag book. You may need to check on some children more frequently than others to ensure they keep up.

This week's word list

on

cat

cot

log

hop

hen

pop

legs

dogs

spots

my

Matching sounds and pictures

1. Say the letter sounds.   2. Say what is in each picture.   3. Draw a line to join the correct letter to its picture.

Classworks: The Synthetic Phonics Book © Helen Hadley, Nelson Thornes Ltd, 2006

Get a Goal

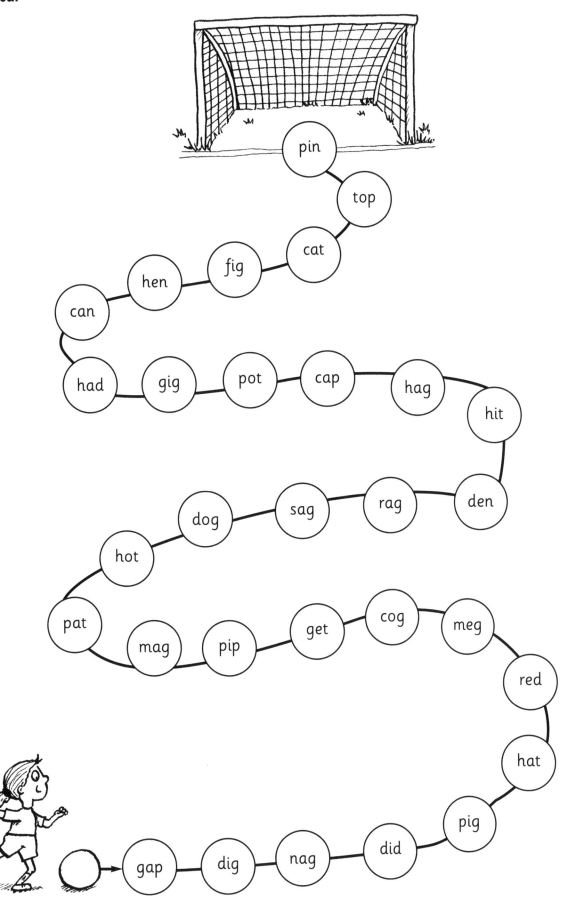

Can you kick them into the net in 1 minute?

Classworks: The Synthetic Phonics Book © Helen Hadley, Nelson Thornes Ltd, 2006

pip is not
a sad dog

5

pip is not
a fat dog

6

I can pat pip

7

pip has a nap

8

pip can dig

4

pip is my pet

3

pip is my dog

2

Week 4
letters: o c g h

my

1

Fold across the middle and make a zigzag book.　　Sound the letters then read the book.

**Week 5
Lesson plan**

| Monday | **u** | Tuesday | **b** | Wednesday | **v** | Thursday | **w** |

Follow this sequence for introducing these letters: **u**, **b**, **v**, **w**.

Remind children that the more letters they learn, the more words they can read.

Identifying the sound

- Hold up items or pictures of items beginning with the day's letter.
- Ask the children what the items are.
- What sound can they hear at the beginning of each word?
- What can they tell you about these words? Yes, they all begin with the same sound. What sound is that?
- Say words beginning with the new sound; children say the word, then the sound it begins with.
- Is there anyone in the class whose name begins with this sound? Do they know anyone else whose name begins with the sound?
- Can they think of other words beginning with the day's sound?
- Say sentences with some words in them beginning with the day's sound, and ask them to tell you which words begin with that sound.
- Create a 'sound' table with a few items beginning with the letter. Children add things they find or bring from home beginning with the sound. Throughout the week add to the letter table, then send items home at the end of each week.
- Hang up the new letters. Use them in daily ten-minute sessions.

Making the sound

Take time to practise the correct way to pronounce each sound with the children.

- /u/ is a hard sound at the back of the mouth with an open mouth.
- /b/ is made by pressing the lips together then releasing them quickly.
- /v/ is made by biting the bottom lip and then letting go.
- /w/ is by pursing the lips and then opening them.

Learning the sound

- Say it loudly, say it softly, say it rhythmically, say it slowly and then say it quickly several times.
- Hold up or point to pictures of things beginning with the day's letter. Emphasise the vowel, e.g. buuun – 'bun' etc. Keep the /b/, /v/ and /w/ sounds short, pure sounds not /buh/ or /ber/, /vuh/ or /ver/, /wuh/ or /wer/.
- Use the large, laminated letters (from the ten-minute sessions) and hold up the one with today's letter on it, saying, "This is today's letter. It is … What does it say? Yes, it says …"
- Put it with a few other letters and show them to the children. Ask them to put their hands up as soon as they see today's letter.
- Write words using known letters and ask, "What does this word say?"
- Use short sentences containing this week's letters.

Writing the new letter

Do this section with the children sitting at their tables with crayons, pencils and paper in front of them.

- Draw the day's letter on the board as large as you can, saying the letter as you write it.
- Facing the children, tell them to stand up.
- Say the letter slowly as you draw a huge mirror image of its shape right across your body with a pointing finger. Now ask the children to do it with you. By facing the children you can see whether they are starting in the right place and shaping the letter correctly. Stretch up, bend, reaching from side to side, use all your body space to make the letter really huge.
- Do this several times together and separately. Check that they are forming the shape correctly.
- Ask them to sit down and draw the letter's shape with their finger on the table top saying its sound at the same time.
- Let them cover the paper with the letter, writing it in pencil and with crayons of different colours, writing it big, writing it small.
- Walk round and check that the children are using a triangular pencil grip, and correct as necessary.

Worksheet activities

Children use the worksheet for the day's letter to reinforce how to:

1 form the letter – go over it with a finger, then several times with both pencil and crayons; (Draw a replica of the shape on the board and show children how to follow the arrows to complete the word.)
2 write the letter – trace over the printed letters, then write it between the lines;
3 find the letter – circle the correct letter for the top line of pictures;
4 write the words for the bottom line of pictures.

If you have a classroom assistant or helper they should repeat the session later in the day for reinforcement with slow learners (or those who have been absent).

Star word:

- Hold up the star word and ask if anyone knows the word.
- Say the word and ask the children to repeat it.
- Ask them why star words are different. Remind them that they are tricky words; words they have to know by looking at them, not by trying to build them.
- Say sentences with the word 'the' in them. Ask them to make up some for you.
- Hang up the star word and refer back to it at times during each day when you or they use the word, so they hear it in common usage.

Classworks Synthetic Phonics Photocopiable Readers

The following Photocopiable Readers can be used this week:

- lost in the fog
- my dog vic
- on the raft
- sand in dad's van.

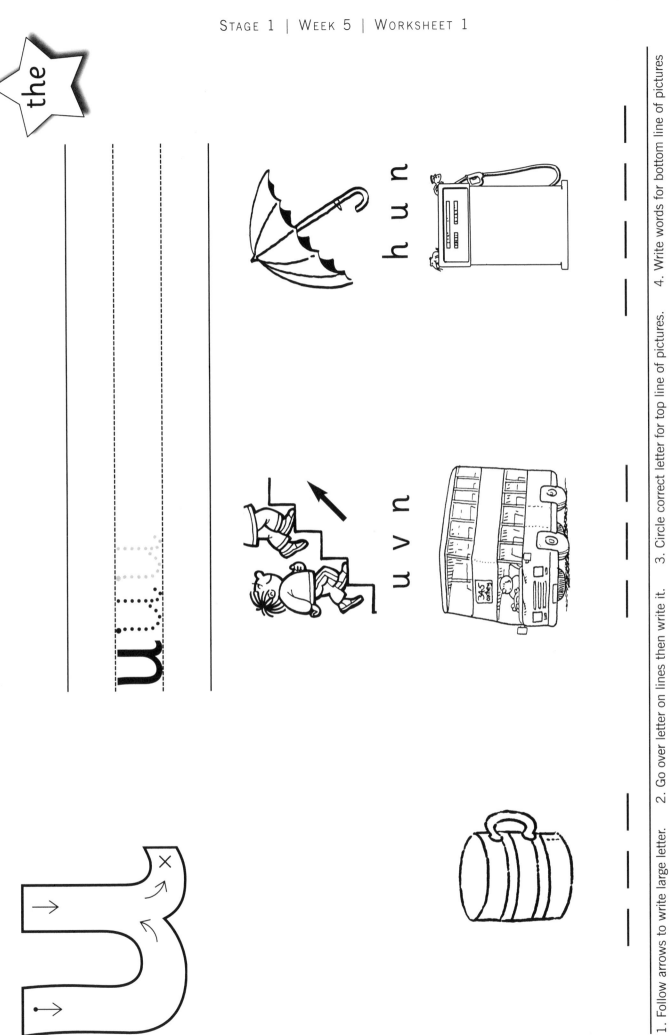

the

u

h u n

u v n

1. Follow arrows to write large letter.   2. Go over letter on lines then write it.   3. Circle correct letter for top line of pictures.   4. Write words for bottom line of pictures

Classworks: The Synthetic Phonics Book © Helen Hadley, Nelson Thornes Ltd, 2006

the

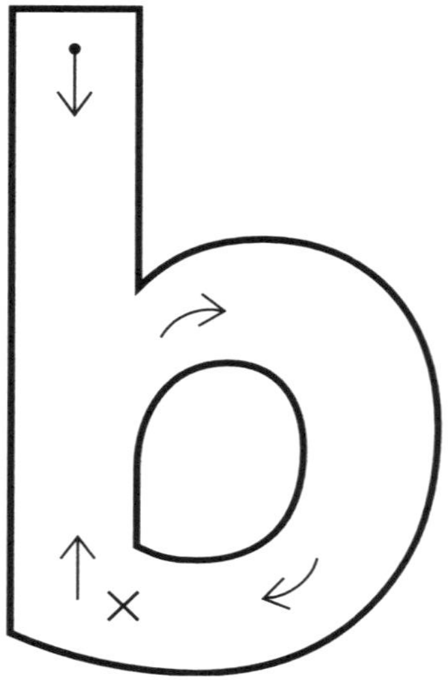

b

b h p

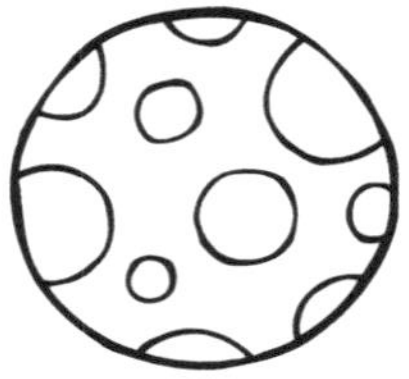

d a b

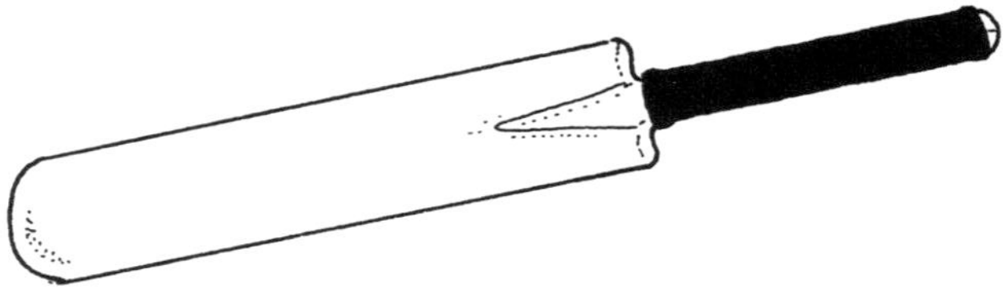

1. Follow arrows to write large letter.   2. Go over letter on lines then write it.   3. Circle correct letter for top line of pictures.   4. Write words for bottom line of pictures

Classworks: The Synthetic Phonics Book © Helen Hadley Nelson Thornes Ltd 2006

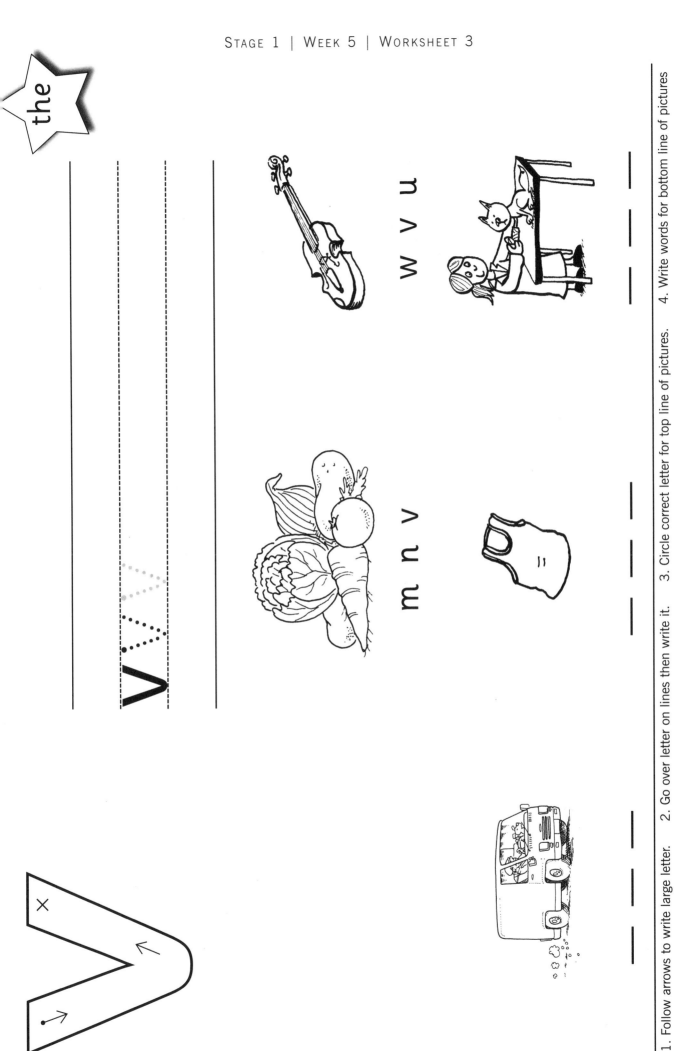

the

v

m n v

w v u

=

1. Follow arrows to write large letter.   2. Go over letter on lines then write it.   3. Circle correct letter for top line of pictures.   4. Write words for bottom line of pictures

Classworks: *The Synthetic Phonics Book* © Helen Hadley, Nelson Thornes Ltd, 2006

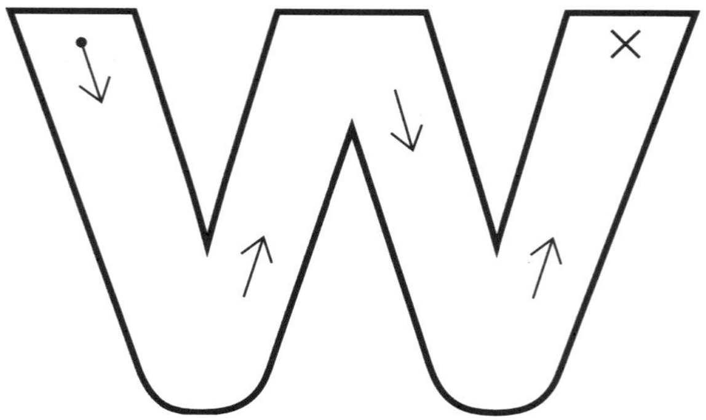

the

X

w

w m u

v w u

1. Follow arrows to write large letter.　2. Go over letter on lines then write it.　3. Circle correct letter for top line of pictures.　4. Write words for bottom line of pictures.

Classworks: The Synthetic Phonics Book © Helen Hadley Nelson Thornes Ltd 2006

Week 5
Friday review

Preparation

- Have ready the laminated cards of letters learnt to date.

Revision

- Holding up each of this week's letters in turn, you say, "This is **u**. What is it?" The children say the sound of the letter.
- Go through the letters for the children to respond to, getting faster and faster.
- Give out three copies of letters learnt to date, and have a copy of each yourself.
- Holding up one of this week's letters ask, "What is this letter?" They respond. "If you have letter **u**, hold it up." Do this for all of this week's letters several times.
- Say one of this week's letters and invite someone to come and write that letter on the board. Do this for all of this week's letters several times.
- Using the word list, ask the children to come out if they have any of the letters for a word you give them, e.g. hold up the letters for the word 'up'. "What does this word say? Come out if you have any of the letters for the word 'up'."
- Using the word list for reference, say a word and ask the children to come out if they have any of the letters from that word.
- Use the letter fans for this week's letters for word-building activities – see games and activities, page 5.
- The word lists can also be used to check the progress of individual children.
- Each week, select a few children to check their progress on the minute tracks and to hear them read the zigzag book. You may need to check on some children more frequently than others to ensure they keep up.

This week's word list

up	van
cup	bus
bun	mugs
nut	drum
rug	the
wag	

Matching sounds and pictures

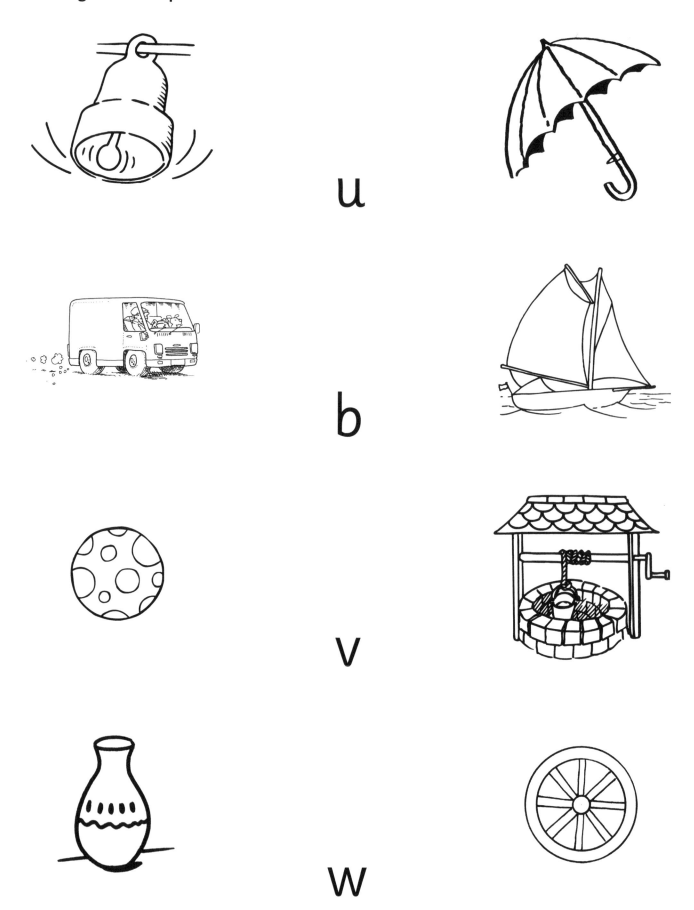

1. Say the letter sounds.   2. Say what is in each picture.   3. Draw a line to join the correct letter to its picture.

Classworks: The Synthetic Phonics Book © Helen Hadley, Nelson Thornes Ltd, 2006

Party-time

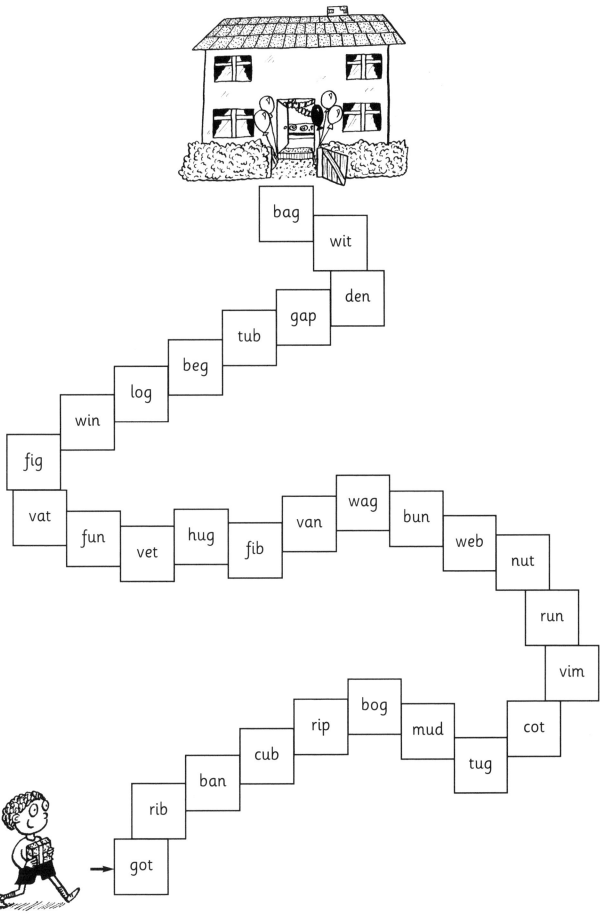

Can you get to the party in 1 minute?

Classworks: The Synthetic Phonics Book © Helen Hadley, Nelson Thornes Ltd, 2006

my dog is in
the van

4

my cat is not
in the van

5

my mum is in
the van

3

my dad, my
mum and my
dog

6

my dad has a
big van

2

and I went to
my nan's

7

Week 5
letters: u b v w

the

1

it is hot in
the sun

8

Fold across the middle and make a zigzag book.   Sound the letters then read the book.

72

Week 6
Lesson plan

Monday	**k**	Tuesday	**y**	Wednesday	**j**	Thursday	**z**

Follow this sequence for introducing these letters: **k**, **y**, **j**, **z**.

Remind children that the more letters they learn, the more words they can read.

Identifying the sound

- Hold up items or pictures of items beginning with the day's letter.
- Ask the children what the items are.
- What sound can they hear at the beginning of each word?
- What can they tell you about these words? Yes, they all begin with the same sound. What sound is that?
- Say words beginning with the new sound; children say the word, then the sound it begins with.
- Is there anyone in the class whose name begins with this sound? Do they know anyone else whose name begins with the sound?
- Can they think of other words beginning with the day's sound?
- Say sentences with some words in them beginning with the day's sound, and ask them to tell you which words begin with that sound.
- Create a 'sound' table with a few items beginning with the letter. Children add things they find or bring from home beginning with the sound. Throughout the week add to the letter table, then send items home at the end of each week.
- Hang up the new letters. Use them in daily ten-minute sessions.

Making the sound

Take time to practise the correct way to pronounce each sound with the children.

- /k/ is made with a clicking sound in the back of the throat.
- /y/ is made by having the mouth slightly open and suddenly dropping the jaw.
- /j/ is made squeezing the cheeks into the mouth and pursing the lips.
- /z/ is made by closing the teeth and buzzing like a fly.

Learning the sound

- Say it loudly, say it softly, say it rhythmically, say it slowly and then say it quickly several times.
- Hold up or point to pictures of things beginning with the day's letter. Emphasise the vowel, e.g. kiiiit for 'kit'. Keep the /k/, /y/, /j/, /z/ sounds short, pure sounds not /kuh/ or /ker/, /yuh/, /juh/ or /zuh/.
- Use the large, laminated letters (from the ten-minute sessions) and hold up the one with today's letter on it, saying, "This is today's letter. It is … What does it say? Yes, it says …"
- Put it with a few other letters and show them to the children. Ask them to put their hands up as soon as they see today's letter.
- Write words using known letters and ask, "What does this word say?"
- Use short sentences containing this week's letters.

Writing the new letter

Do this section with the children sitting at their tables with crayons, pencils and paper in front of them.

- Draw the day's letter on the board as large as you can, saying the letter as you write it.
- Facing the children, tell them to stand up.
- Say the letter slowly as you draw a huge mirror image of its shape right across your body with a pointing finger. Now ask the children to do it with you. By facing the children you can see whether they are starting in the right place and shaping the letter correctly. Stretch up, bend, reaching from side to side, use all your body space to make the letter really huge.
- Do this several times together and separately. Check that they are forming the shape correctly.
- Ask them to sit down and draw the letter's shape with their finger on the table top saying its sound at the same time.
- Let them cover the paper with the letter, writing it in pencil and with crayons of different colours, writing it big, writing it small.
- Walk round and check that the children are using a triangular pencil grip, and correct as necessary.

Worksheet activities

Children use the worksheet for the day's letter to reinforce how to:

1 form the letter – go over it with a finger, then several times with both pencil and crayons; (Draw a replica of the shape on the board and show children how to follow the arrows to complete the word.)
2 write the letter – trace over the printed letters, then write it between the lines;
3 find the letter – circle the correct letter for the top line of pictures;
4 write the words for the bottom line of pictures.

If you have a classroom assistant or helper they should repeat the session later in the day for reinforcement with slow learners (or those who have been absent).

Star word:

- Hold up the star word and ask if anyone knows the word.
- Say the word and ask the children to repeat it.
- Ask them why star words are different. Remind them that they are tricky words; words they have to know by looking at them, not by trying to build them.
- Say sentences with the word 'to' in them. Ask them to make up some for you.
- Hang up the star word and refer back to it at times during each day when you or they use the word, so they hear it in common usage.

Classworks Synthetic Phonics Photocopiable Readers

The following Photocopiable Readers can be used this week:

- kip and the bun
- jim and viv and the milk
- skip at the vet's
- my zig-zag.

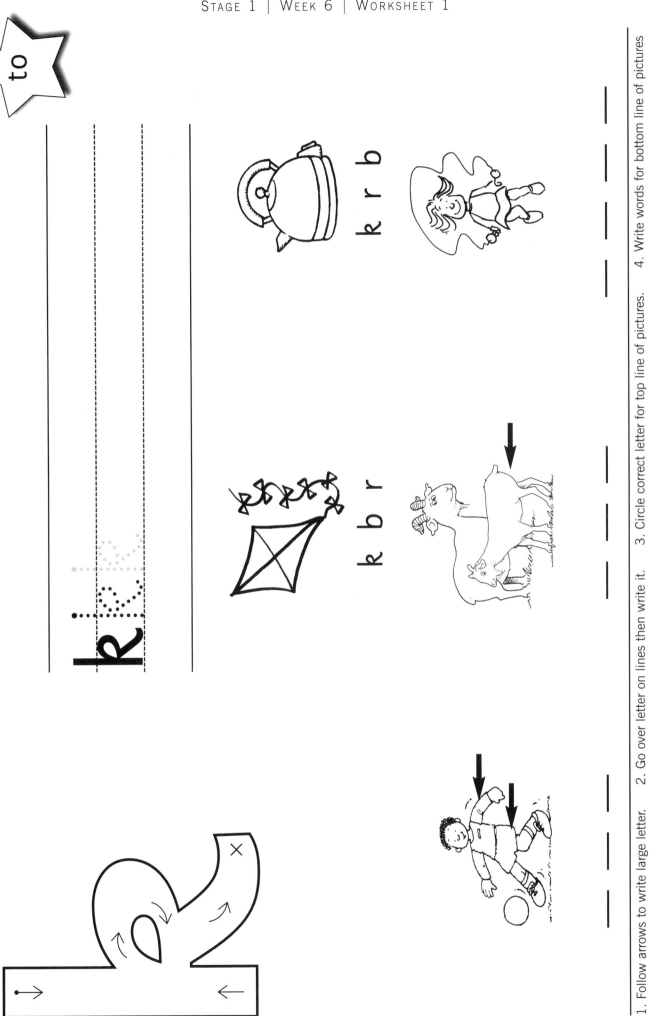

to

k r b

k b r

1. Follow arrows to write large letter.   2. Go over letter on lines then write it.   3. Circle correct letter for top line of pictures.   4. Write words for bottom line of pictures

Classworks: The Synthetic Phonics Book © Helen Hadley, Nelson Thornes Ltd, 2006

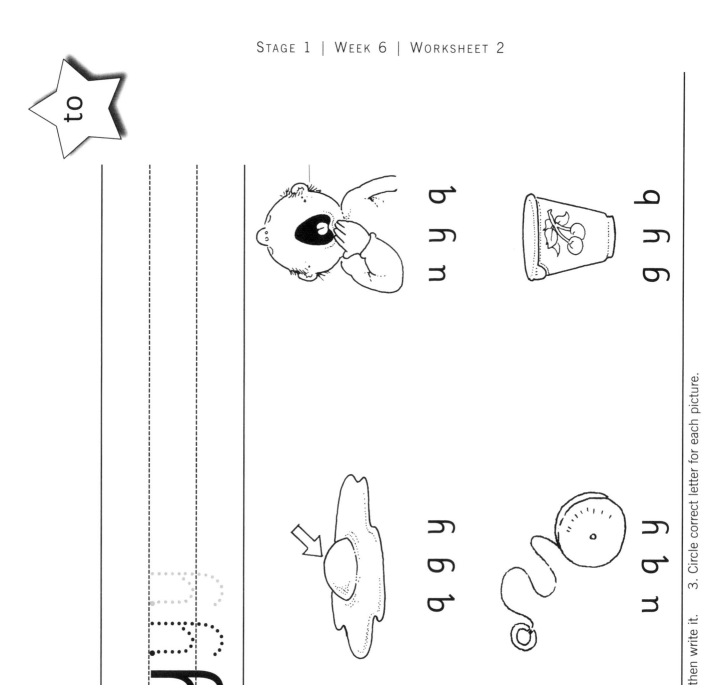

b h n

h g b

q h g

h b n

h b g

1. Follow arrows to write large letter.   2. Go over letter on lines then write it.   3. Circle correct letter for each picture.

to

j i b

g j

j

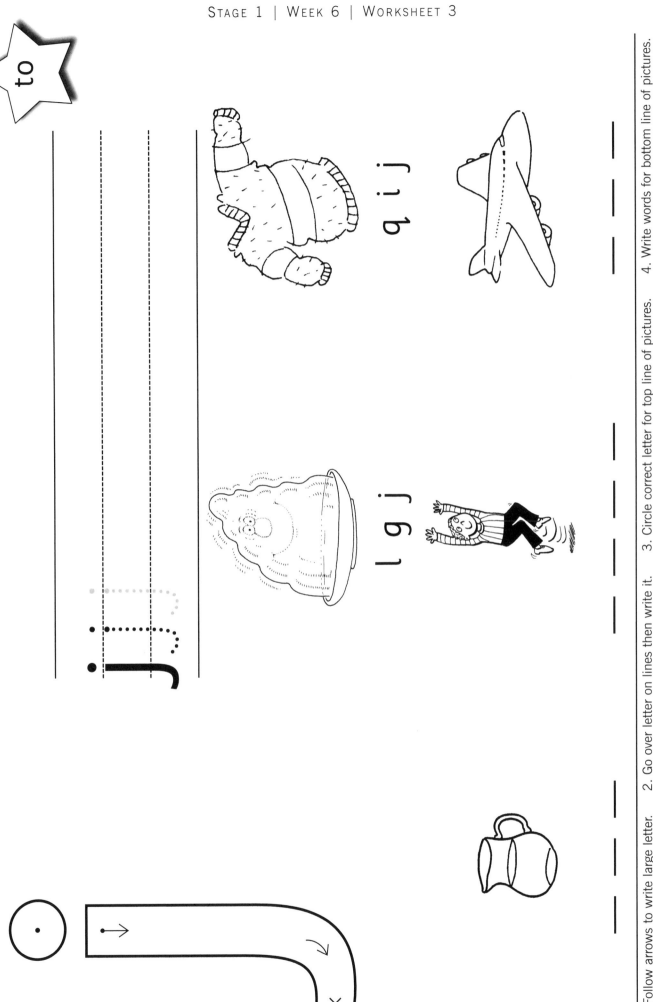

77

1. Follow arrows to write large letter.   2. Go over letter on lines then write it.   3. Circle correct letter for top line of pictures.   4. Write words for bottom line of pictures.

Classworks: The Synthetic Phonics Book © Helen Hadley, Nelson Thornes Ltd, 2006

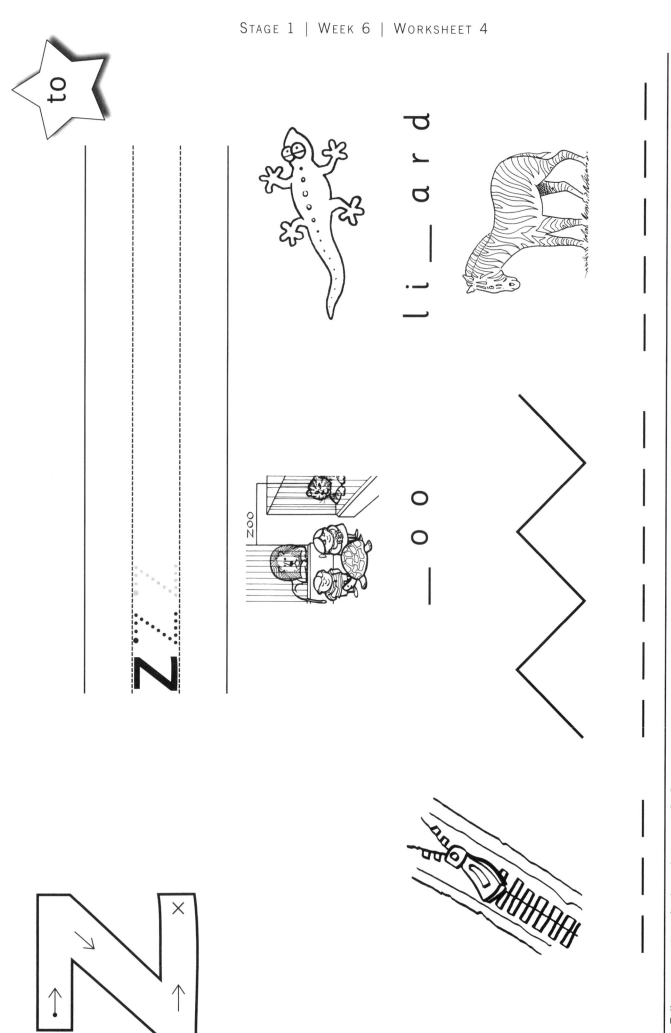

to

li_ard

_oo

N

1. Follow arrows to write large letter.   2. Go over letter on lines then write it.   3. Write the word for the picture.

Week 6
Friday review

Preparation

- Have ready the laminated cards of letters learnt to date.

Revision

- Holding up each of this week's letters in turn, you say, "This is **k**. What is it?" The children say the sound of the letter.
- Go through the letters for the children to respond to, getting faster and faster.
- Give out three copies of letters learnt to date, and have a copy of each yourself.
- Holding up one of this week's letters ask, "What is this letter?" They respond. "If you have letter **k**, hold it up." Do this for all of this week's letters several times.
- Say one of this week's letters and invite someone to come and write that letter on the board. Do this for all of this week's letters several times.
- Using the word list, ask the children to come out if they have any of the letters for a word you give them, e.g. hold up the letters for the word 'kit'. "What does this word say? Come out if you have any of the letters for the word 'kit'."
- Using the word list for reference, say a word and ask the children to come out if they have any of the letters from that word.
- Use the letter fans for this week's letters for word-building activities – see games and activities, page 5.
- The word lists can also be used to check the progress of individual children.
- Each week, select a few children to check their progress on the minute tracks and to hear them read the zigzag book. You may need to check on some children more frequently than others to ensure they keep up.

This week's word list

kit	ken
yes	yap
jam	jig
jug	zap
zip	
yelp	

to

Matching sounds and pictures

k

y

j

z

---

1. Say the letter sounds.   2. Say what is in each picture.   3. Draw a line to join the correct letter to its picture.

Classworks: The Synthetic Phonics Book © Helen Hadley, Nelson Thornes Ltd, 2006

Run the Track

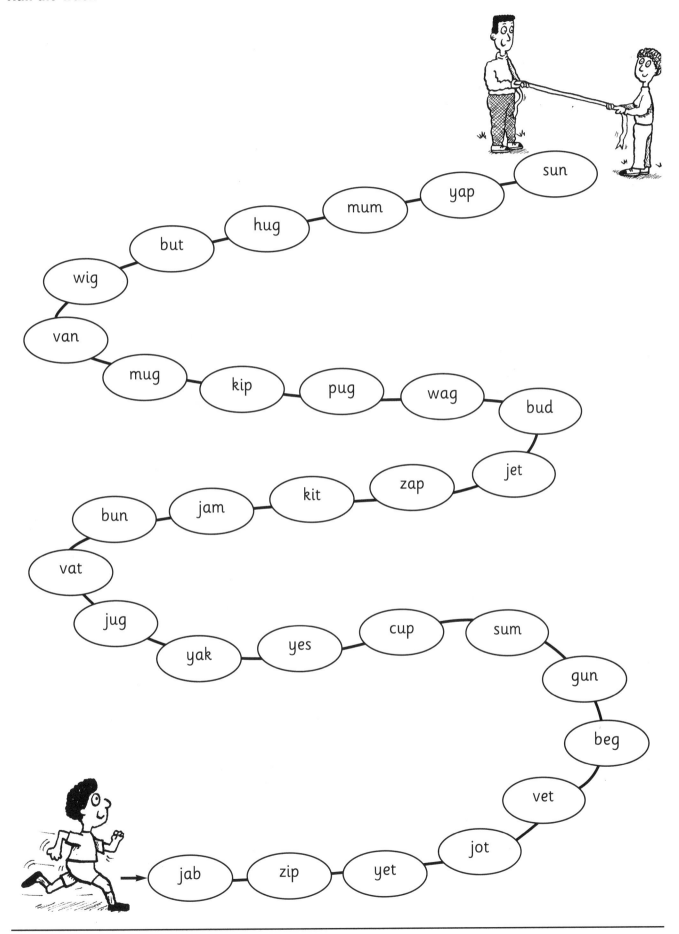

Can you reach the tape in 1 minute?

Classworks: The Synthetic Phonics Book © Helen Hadley, Nelson Thornes Ltd, 2006

4

I had to get
my bag and
my kit

5

my mum, my
dad and I
went on a jet

3

my mum had
a bag

6

it was a big
red jet

2

my dad had
his bag

7

it went in a
zig-zag

1

Week 6
letters: k y j z

to

8

it is fun in a
jet

Fold across the middle and make a zigzag book.   Sound the letters then read the book.

Stage 2 – Weeks 7–9

**Week 7
Lesson plan**

Monday	**ch**	Tuesday	**sh**	Wednesday	**th**	Thursday	**tch**

Follow this sequence for introducing these consonant clusters: **ch**, **sh**, **th**, **tch**.

Identifying the sound

- Hold up items or pictures of items containing the day's consonant cluster.
- Ask the children what the items are.
- What sound is the same in each word?
- Is there anyone in the class whose name has this sound in it? Do they know anyone else whose name has the sound in it?
- Can they think of other words with the day's sound in them?
- Say sentences with some words in them using the day's sound and ask them to tell you in which words that sound is used.
- Hang up the consonant clusters. Use them in daily ten-minute sessions.

Making the sound

Take time to practise the correct way to pronounce each sound with the children.

- /ch/ is made by pushing the lips out as you make the sound of a steam train.
- /sh/ is made by pushing the lips out and breathing out through closed teeth.
- /th/ is made by placing the tongue between the teeth and pulling it in quickly.
- /tch/ is made the same way as /ch/.

Note: th has two sounds. One is the unvoiced sound, made by placing the tongue between the teeth and pulling it in quickly, as in 'moth', 'think' etc. The other is the voiced sound, made with the tongue lying at the bottom of the mouth, as in 'that', 'them', 'then', 'this', 'with', 'smooth', 'clothe' etc.
In this lesson plan we have focused on the unvoiced sound.

Learning the sound

- Say it loudly, say it softly, say it rhythmically, say it slowly and then say it quickly several times.
- Hold up or point to pictures of things containing the day's consonant cluster. Emphasise the vowel sounds in the word, e.g. chiiip – 'chip' etc.
- Keep the /ch/, /sh/ and /th/ sounds short, pure sounds not /chuh/, /shuh/, /thuh/.

Writing the sound

- Standing up, revise the writing of the consonant cluster's shape.
- Ask the children to sit down and draw the consonant cluster's shape with their finger on the table, saying its sound at the same time.
- Ask them to cover the paper with the letters, writing in pencil, with crayons of different colours, writing big, writing small.

Worksheet activities

- Give out the worksheet and ask the children to form the letters in the consonant cluster by following the arrows – going over it with a finger; then several times with both pencil and crayons.
- Ask them to put a ring round all the consonant clusters on the page which match the one they have traced.
- Ask them to look at each picture, think of its sounds. Draw a line to match the word to its picture.
- Build words from the given consonant clusters and letters. Write them in the empty box.

Star word:

- Hold up the star word and ask if anyone knows the word.
- Say the word and ask the children to repeat it.
- Ask them why star words are different. Remind them that they are tricky words; words they have to know by looking at them, not by trying to build them.
- Say sentences with the word 'of' in them. Ask them to make up some for you.
- Hang up the star word and refer back to it at times during each day when you or they use the word, so they hear it in common usage.

Classworks Synthetic Phonics Photocopiable Readers

The following Photocopiable Readers can be used this week:

- dad's shed
- patch has an itch
- my big fish
- the rich jam buns.

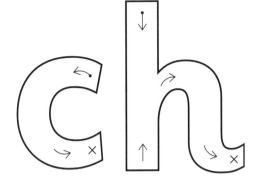

ch	sh	hc	ch	hs	ch

chips

bunch

bench

chin

		ch
b	e	
		nch
ch	i	
		p
m	o	
		st
r	u	

1. Follow arrows to write letters.   2. Ring the **ch** letter clusters.   3. Match the words to the pictures.
4. Build **ch** words from the given letters and write them in the box.

Classworks: The Synthetic Phonics Book © Helen Hadley, Nelson Thornes Ltd, 2006

sh	hs	ch	sh	hs	sh

ship

brush

sh

fish

shop

d		lf	
	e		
f		ll	
	i		
sh		p	
	o		
		sh	

1. Follow arrows to write letters.   2. Ring the **sh** letter clusters.   3. Match the words to the pictures.
4. Build **sh** words from the given letters and write them in the box.

Classworks: The Synthetic Phonics Book © Helen Hadley, Nelson Thornes Ltd, 2006

of

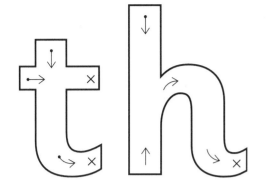

th	ht	th	sh	hc	th

moth

thump

th

$1 + 4 = 5$

$2 + 1 = 3$

$3 + 3 = 6$

maths

cloth

cl a e i th o	n s th	

1. Follow arrows to write letters.   2. Ring the **th** letter clusters.   3. Match the words to the pictures.
4. Build **th** words from the given letters and write them in the box.

Classworks: The Synthetic Phonics Book © Helen Hadley, Nelson Thornes Ltd, 2006

tch	cth	htc	tch	tch	tch

latch

witch

tch

hatch

hutch

b		
c	a	
h	i	tch
p	u	
w		

1. Follow arrows to write letters.   2. Ring the **tch** letter clusters.   3. Match the words to the pictures.
4. Build **tch** words from the given letters and write them in the box.

Classworks: The Synthetic Phonics Book © Helen Hadley, Nelson Thornes Ltd, 2006

Week 7
Friday review

Preparation

- Have ready the laminated cards of letters learnt to date.

Revision

- Holding up each of this week's consonant clusters in turn, you say, "This is **ch**. What is it?" The children say the sound.
- The children respond to the consonant clusters as you go through them, getting faster and faster.
- Give out three copies of this week's consonant clusters, plus all the letters learnt to date, and have a copy of each for yourself.
- Hold up a consonant cluster and ask, "What is this sound?" They respond. "If you have the same sound, hold it up." Do this for all of this week's sounds several times.
- Say one of this week's consonant clusters and invite someone to come and write it on the board. Do this for all of this week's consonant clusters several times.
- Using the word list, ask the children to come out if they have any of the letters for a word you give them, e.g. hold up the letters for the word 'chips'. "What does this word say? Come out if you have any of the letters for the word 'chips'."
- Using the word list for reference, say a word and ask the children to come out if they have any of the letters from that word.
- Use the letter fans of letters learnt to date for word-building activities – see games and activities, page 5.
- The word lists can also be used to check the progress of individual children.
- Each week, select a few children to check their progress on the minute tracks and to hear them read the zigzag book. You may need to check on some children more frequently than others to ensure they keep up.

This week's word list

chop	pith
chum	think
rich	fetch
shut	patch
cash	of

89

Complete the words

__ __ o p   c a __ __ __

m o __ __   __ __ i p s

th

b e n __ __   b r u __ __

tch

w i __ __ __   c l o __ __

Fill in the missing letters to complete the words.

Find the right word

Picture	Words	Picture	Words
	chops chips chimps		crush brush brash
	ship shop shut		crunch bench bunch
	think thank thump		batch patch latch
	hutch ditch stitch		moth maths pith
	chest chin chip		dish wish fish

1. Say what is in the picture.   2. Read all three words.   3. Circle the right word.

Classworks: The Synthetic Phonics Book © Helen Hadley, Nelson Thornes Ltd, 2006

Get a Goal

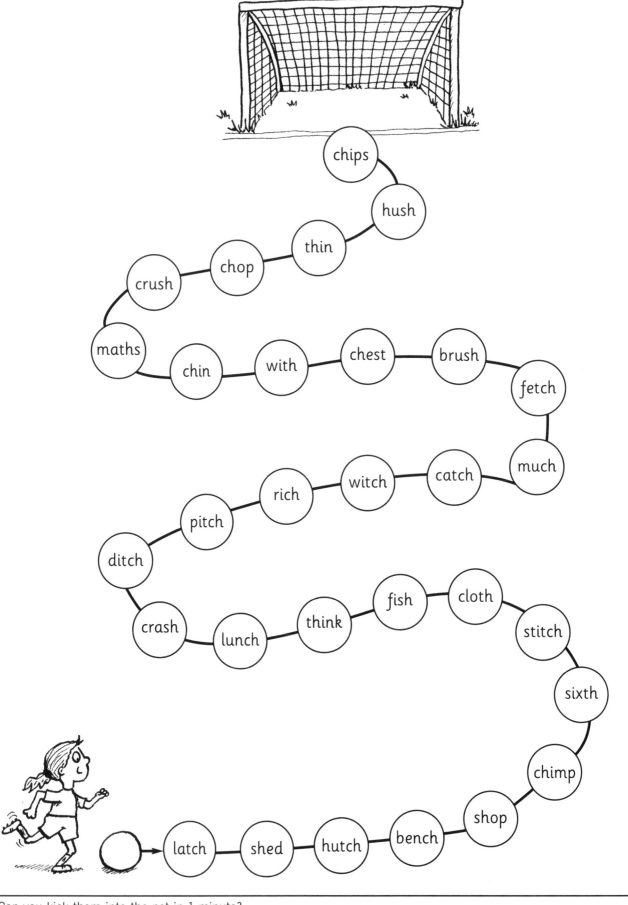

Can you kick them into the net in 1 minute?

Classworks: The Synthetic Phonics Book © Helen Hadley, Nelson Thornes Ltd, 2006

chad and I
went to the
shop to get
lunch

4

chad and I
ran to the
pond with
the lunch

5

I had a bit of
cash

3

my chum and
I sat on a
bench to
munch lunch

6

chad is my
chum

2

I had chips
for my lunch

7

Week 7

letters:
ch sh th tch

of

1

I dip my
chips in
ketchup

8

Fold across the middle and make a zigzag book.   Sound the letters then read the book.

93

Classworks: The Synthetic Phonics Book © Helen Hadley, Nelson Thornes Ltd, 2006

Week 8
Lesson plan

Monday	**ck**	Tuesday	**ss**	Wednesday	**ll**	Thursday	**ff**

Follow this sequence for introducing these digraphs: **ck**, **ss**, **ll**, **ff**.

Identifying the sound

- Hold up items or pictures of items containing the day's consonant cluster.
- Ask the children what the items are.
- What sound is the same in each word?
- Is there anyone in the class whose name has this sound in it? Do they know anyone else whose name has the sound in it?
- Can they think of other words with the day's sound in them?
- Say sentences with some words in them using the day's sound, and ask them to tell you in which words that sound is used.
- Hang up the digraphs. Use them in daily ten-minute sessions.

Making the sound

Take time to practise the correct way to pronounce each sound with the children.

- /ck/ is a hard sound made at the back of the throat.
- /ss/ is made by breathing out through closed teeth.
- /ll/ is made by curling the tongue against the roof of the mouth.
- /ff/ is made by biting the lower lip and breathing out.

Learning the sound

- Say it loudly, say it softly, say it rhythmically, say it slowly and then say it quickly several times.
- Hold up or point to pictures of things containing the day's consonant cluster. Emphasise the vowel sounds in the word, e.g. baaack – 'back' etc.
- Keep the /ck/, /ss/, /ll/ and /ff/ as pure sounds not /ckuh/, /suh/, /luh/ or /fuh/.

Writing the sound

- Standing up, revise the writing of the consonant cluster's shape.
- Ask the children to sit down and draw the consonant cluster's shape with their finger on the table, saying its sound at the same time.
- Ask them to cover the paper with the consonant cluster, writing in pencil, with crayons of different colours, writing big, writing small.

Worksheet activities

- Give out the worksheet and ask the children to form the letters in the consonant cluster by following the arrows – going over it with a finger; then several times with both pencil and crayons.
- Ask them to put a ring round all the consonant clusters on the page which match the one they have traced.
- Ask them to look at each picture and think of its sounds. Draw a line to match the word to its picture.
- Build words from the given consonant clusters and letters. Write them in the empty box.

Star word:

- Hold up the star word and ask if anyone knows the word.
- Say the word and ask the children to repeat it.
- Ask them why star words are different. Remind them that they are tricky words; words they have to know by looking at them, not by trying to build them.
- Say sentences with the word 'was' in them. Ask them to make up some for you.
- Hang up the star word and refer back to it at times during each day when you or they use the word, so they hear it in common usage.

Classworks Synthetic Phonics Photocopiable Readers

The following Photocopiable Readers can be used this week:

- lunch on the rocks
- lunch at the mill
- the doll and the duck
- bad zack.

was

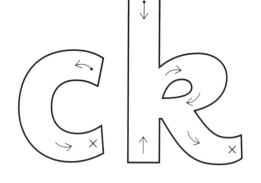

ek	ck	ok	ck	ek	ck

clock

duck

ck

bricks

truck

a		
cl		
	i	
s		ck
	o	
tr		
	u	

1. Follow arrows to write letters.   2. Ring the **ck** letter clusters.   3. Match the words to the pictures.
4. Build **ck** words from the given letters and write them in the box.

Classworks: The Synthetic Phonics Book © Helen Hadley, Nelson Thornes Ltd, 2006

SS

| ss | zz | ee | ss | cs | ss |

cross

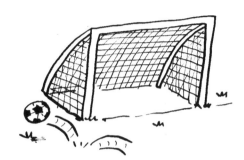

kiss

ss

miss

dress

cr		
	e	
dr		
	i	ss
l		
	o	
m		

1. Follow arrows to write letters.   2. Ring the **ss** letter clusters.   3. Match the words to the pictures.
4. Build **ss** words from the given letters and write them in the box.

Classworks: The Synthetic Phonics Book © Helen Hadley, Nelson Thornes Ltd, 2006

was

| lt | ll | tl | ll | ff | ll |

smell

doll

ll

well

bell

b		
	e	
d		ll
	i	
f		
	o	
w		

1. Follow arrows to write letters.   2. Ring the **ll** letter clusters.   3. Match the words to the pictures.
4. Build **ll** words from the given letters and write them in the box.

Classworks: The Synthetic Phonics Book © Helen Hadley, Nelson Thornes Ltd, 2006

was

fr	ff	fl	tf	ff	ff

ff

cliff

muff

sniff

cuff

c		
	i	
h		
		ff
m		
	u	
sn		
st		

1. Follow arrows to write letters.   2. Ring the **ff** letter clusters.   3. Match the words to the pictures.
4. Build **ff** words from the given letters and write them in the box.

Classworks: The Synthetic Phonics Book © Helen Hadley, Nelson Thornes Ltd, 2006

Week 8
Friday review

Preparation

- Have ready the laminated cards of letters learnt to date.

Revision

- Holding up each of this week's digraphs in turn, you say, "This is **ck**. What is it?" The children say the sound.
- The children respond to the digraphs as you go through them, getting faster and faster.
- Give out three copies of this week's digraphs, plus all the letters learnt to date, and have a copy of each for yourself.
- Hold up a digraph and ask, "What is this sound?" They respond. "If you have the same sound, hold it up." Do this for all of this week's sounds several times.
- Say one of this week's digraphs and invite someone to come and write it on the board.
- Do this for all of this week's digraphs several times.
- Using the word list, ask the children to come out if they have any of the letters for a word you give them, e.g. hold up the letters for the word 'duck'. "What does this word say? Come out if you have any of the letters for the word 'duck'."
- Using the word list for reference, say a word and ask the children to come out if they have any of the letters from that word.
- Use the letter fans of letters learnt to date for word-building activities – see games and activities, page 5.
- The word lists can also be used to check the progress of individual children.
- Each week, select a few children to check their progress on the minute tracks and to hear them read the zigzag book. You may need to check on some children more frequently than others to ensure they keep up.

This week's word list

duck	gull
back	stiff
suck	stuff
rock	chill
less	was
hiss	

Complete the words

s a __ __

l i __ __

c l i __ __

b e __ __

c r o __ __

h i __ __

d r e __ __

c u __ __

Fill in the missing letters to complete the words.

STAGE 2 | WEEK 8 | COPYMASTER 2

Find the right word

	biff cliff tiff	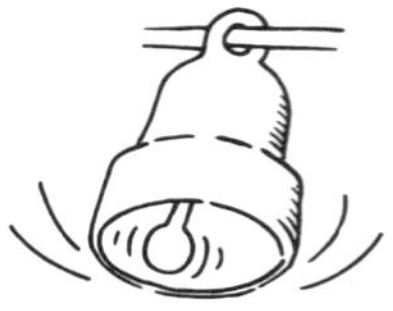	bell tell well
	fill hill bill		cuff buff duff
	loll doll moll		peck deck neck
	rack pack sack		toss cross moss
	tress dress mess		dock sock frock

1. Say what is in the picture. 2. Read all three words. 3. Circle the right word.

102

Party-time

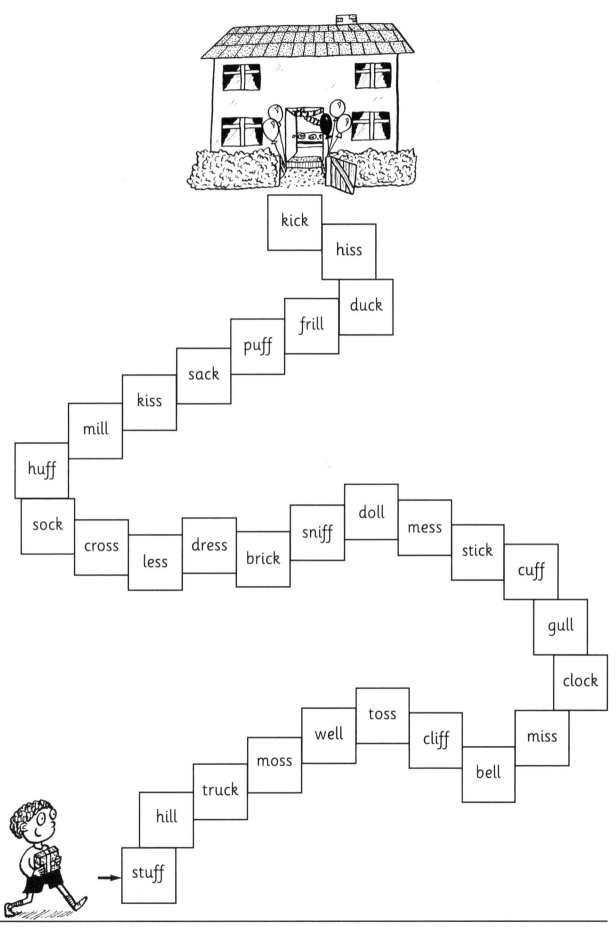

kick

hiss

duck

frill

puff

sack

kiss

mill

huff

sock

cross

less

dress

brick

sniff

doll

mess

stick

cuff

gull

clock

miss

toss

well

cliff

bell

moss

truck

hill

stuff

Can you get to the party in 1 minute?

Classworks: The Synthetic Phonics Book © Helen Hadley, Nelson Thornes Ltd, 2006

5

dad went to
help jill

4

jill fell into
the bucket

6

dad had to
get the
bucket back
to the top

3

the well had
a big bucket

7

dad held jill
with his
hands

2

jill was at the
well on the
cliff

8

dad had a
big kiss from
jill

1

Week 8
letters:
ck ss ll ff

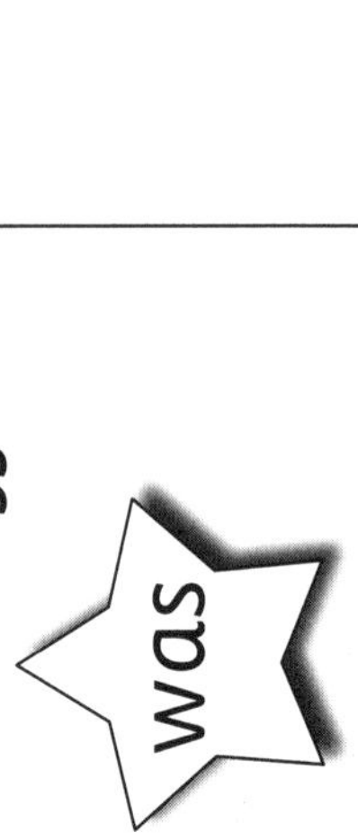

was

104

Fold across the middle and make a zigzag book.   Sound the letters then read the book.

**Week 9
Lesson plan**

| Monday | **qu** | Tuesday | **ng** | Wednesday | **nk** | Thursday | **x** |

Follow this sequence for introducing these letter sounds: **qu**, **ng**, **nk**, **x**.

Identifying the sound

- Hold up items or pictures of items beginning or ending with the day's sound.
- Ask them what the items are.
- What is the same sound in each word?
- Is there anyone in the class whose name has this sound in it? Do they know anyone whose name has the sound in it?
- Can they think of other words with the day's sound in them?
- Say sentences with some words in them using the day's sound and ask them to tell you in which words that sound is used.
- Hang up the new letter sounds. Use them in daily ten-minute sessions.

Making the sound

Take time to practise the correct way to pronounce each sound with the children.

- /qu/ is made by pursing the lips and then widening them as you make the sound.
- /ng/ is made by pressing the tongue against the roof of the mouth and making a humming sound.
- /nk/ is made by pressing the tongue against the roof of the mouth and dropping it as the /k/ sound is made at the back of the throat.
- /x/ is a /k/ sound at the back of the throat coming forward into an /s/ sound.

Learning the sound

- Say it loudly, say it softly, say it rhythmically, say it slowly and then say it quickly several times.
- Hold up or point to pictures of things containing the day's letter. Emphasise the vowel sounds in the word, e.g. booox – 'box' etc.
- Keep the /qu/, /ng/, /nk/ and /x/ sounds short, pure sounds.

Writing the sound

- Standing up, revise the writing of the letters' shapes.
- Ask the children to sit down and draw on the table the shape of the letter and each digraph, saying its sound at the same time.
- Ask them cover the paper with the letter/digraphs, writing in pencil and with crayons of different colours, writing big, writing small.

Worksheet activities

- Give out the worksheet and ask the children to form the letter/digraph by following the arrows – going over it with a finger; then several times with both pencil and crayons.
- Ask them to put a ring round the letter/digraph on the page which matches the one they have traced.
- Ask them to look at each picture and think of its sound. Draw a line to match the word to its picture.
- Build words from the given digraphs and letters. Write them in the empty box.

Star word:

- Hold up the star word and ask if anyone knows the word.
- Say the word and ask the children to repeat it.
- Ask them why star words are different. Remind them that they are tricky words; words they have to know by looking at them, not by trying to build them.
- Say sentences with the word 'for' in them. Ask them to make up some for you.
- Hang up the star word and refer back to it at times during each day when you or they use the word, so they hear it in common usage.

Classworks Synthetic Phonics Photocopiable Readers

The following Photocopiable Readers can be used this week:

- dad and his duck
- the swing
- the bad dog
- jeff's trip.

for

| qu | uq | ug | qu | up | qu |

quilt

quack

qu

quiet

quiff

qu	a	ck
		ll
		lt
	i	t
		z

1. Follow arrows to write letters.   2. Ring the **qu** letter clusters.   3. Match the words to the pictures.
4. Build **gu** words from the given letters and write them in the box.

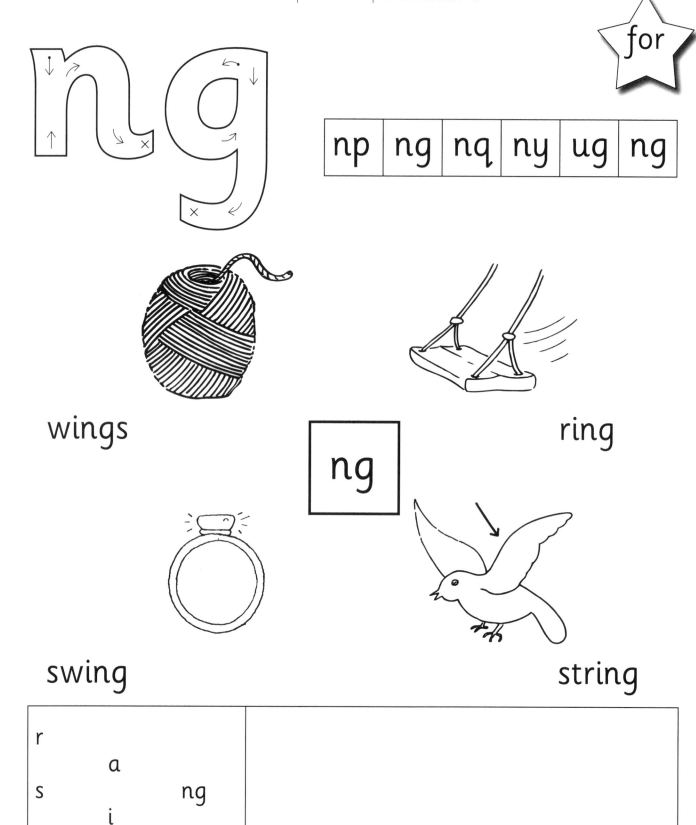

ng

| np | ng | nq | ny | ug | ng |

for

wings

ring

ng

swing

string

r			
	a		
s		ng	
	i		
st			
	u		
sw			

1. Follow arrows to write letters.   2. Ring the **ng** letter clusters.   3. Match the words to the pictures.
4. Build **ng** words from the given letters and write them in the box.

Classworks: The Synthetic Phonics Book © Helen Hadley, Nelson Thornes Ltd, 2006

for

mk	nk	uk	nk	nk	mk

sink

trunk

nk

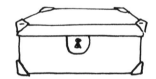

plank

bunk

b			
bl	a		
dr	i	nk	
r	u		
s			

1. Follow arrows to write letters.   2. Ring the **nk** letter clusters.   3. Match the words to the pictures.
4. Build **nk** words from the given letters and write them in the box.

for

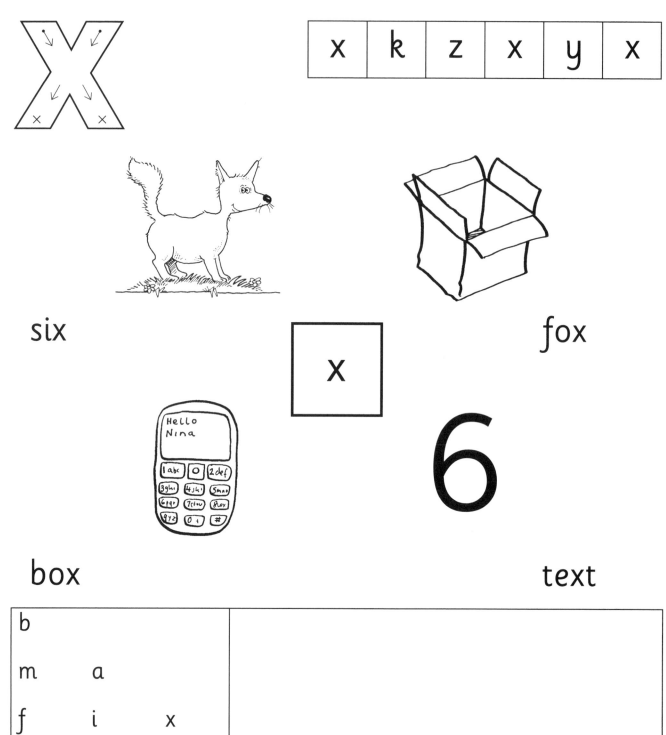

x	k	z	x	y	x

six

x

fox

6

box

text

b		
m	a	
f	i	x
s	o	
w		

1. Follow arrows to write letters.   2. Ring the **x** letter clusters.   3. Match the words to the pictures.
4. Build **x** words from the given letters and write them in the box.

Classworks: The Synthetic Phonics Book © Helen Hadley, Nelson Thornes Ltd, 2006

**Week 9
Friday review**

Preparation

- Have ready the laminated cards of letters learnt to date.

Revision

- Holding up each of this week's sounds in turn, you say, "This is **qu**. What is it?" The children say the sound.
- The children respond to the sounds as you go through them, getting faster and faster.
- Give out three copies of this week's sounds, plus all the letters learnt to date, and have a copy of each for yourself.
- Hold up a sound and ask, "What is this sound?" They respond. "If you have the same sound, hold it up." Do this for all of this week's sounds several times.
- Say one of this week's sounds and invite someone to come and write it on the board.
- Do this for all of this week's sounds several times.
- Using the word list, ask the children to come out if they have any of the letters for a word you give them, e.g. hold up the letters for the word 'quack'. "What does this word say? Come out if you have any of the letters for the word 'quack'."
- Using the word list for reference, say a word and ask the children to come out if they have any of the letters from that word.
- Use the letter fans of letters learnt to date for word-building activities – see games and activities, page 5.
- The word lists can also be used to check the progress of individual children.
- Each week, select a few children to check their progress on the minute tracks and to hear them read the zigzag book. You may need to check on some children more frequently than others to ensure they keep up.

This week's word list

quack	dunk
quill	bank
fang	mix
bring	cox
song	⭐ for
sink	

Complete the words

__ __ i l t

qu

r i __ __

s w i __ __

ng

t h i __ __

s i __ __

nk

d r i __ __

b __ __

x

m __ __

Fill in the missing letters to complete the words.

Classworks: The Synthetic Phonics Book © Helen Hadley, Nelson Thornes Ltd, 2006

Find the right word

	brink rink trunk	
6	mix six fix	
	sink slink links	
	sings wings clings	
	text next tex	
	quilt	quins quit
	hank	bank tank
	bring	swung swing
	box	cox fox
	rang	rung ring

1. Say what is in the picture.   2. Read all three words.   3. Circle the right word.

Run the Track

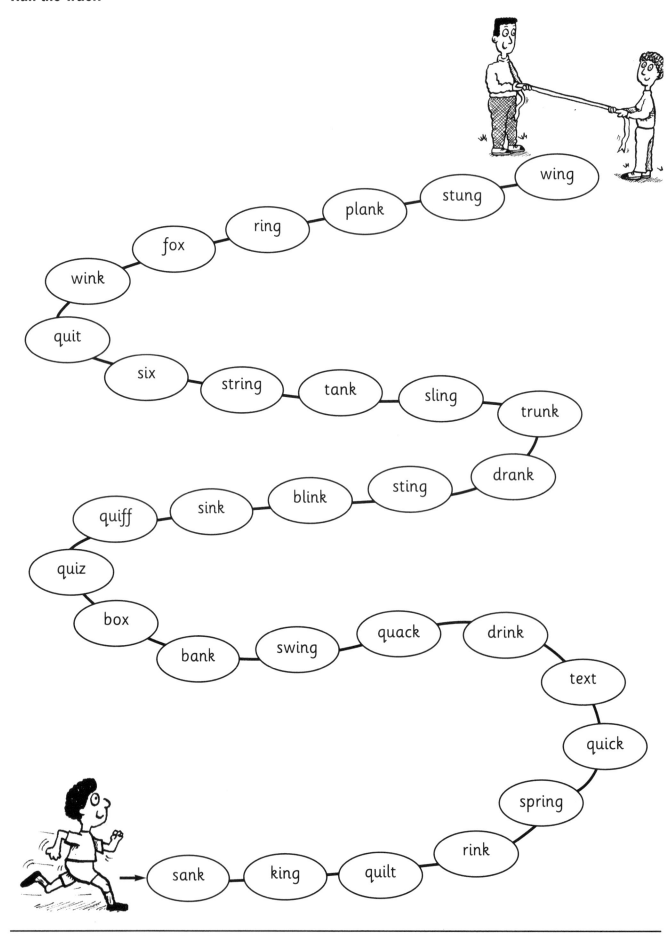

Can you reach the tape in 1 minute?

5

in the box
was a ring

4

the box was
open

6

I went back
to my mum

3

a box was on
the grass

7

I think the
ring is my
gran's

2

I went for a
quick run

8

gran was
glad to get
her ring back

1

Week 9

letters:

qu ng nk x

for

Fold across the middle and make a zigzag book.   Sound the letters then read the book.

Classworks: The Synthetic Phonics Book © Helen Hadley, Nelson Thornes Ltd, 2006

Stage 3 – Weeks 10–12

**Week 10
Lesson plan**

| Monday | a–e | Tuesday | i–e | Wednesday | o–e | Thursday | u–e |

Follow this sequence to introduce these long vowels: **a–e**, **i–e**, **o–e**, **u–e**.

Identifying the sound

- Hold up items or pictures of items containing the day's long vowel.
- Ask the children what the items are.
- What sound is the same in each word?
- Is there anyone in the class whose name has this sound in it? Do they know anyone else whose name has the sound in it?
- Can they think of other words with the day's sound in them?
- Say sentences with some words in them using the day's sound, and ask them to tell you in which words that sound is used.
- Hang up the new long vowels. Use them in daily ten-minute sessions.

Making the sound

Take time to practise the correct way to pronounce each sound with the children.

- **a–e** makes the long vowel sound – say 'ay', the **e** is silent.
- **i–e** makes the long vowel sound – say 'I', the **e** is silent.
- **o–e** makes the long vowel sound – say 'oh', the **e** is silent.
- **u–e** makes the long vowel sound – say 'you', the **e** is silent.

Learning the sound

- Say it loudly, say it softly, say it rhythmically, say it slowly and then say it quickly several times.
- Hold up or point to pictures of things containing the day's long vowel. Emphasise the long vowel sound in the word – e.g. snay–k, 'snake' etc.
- Keep the /ay/, /i/, /oh/ and /you/ sounds long and the consonants short.
- Hold up a word with the long vowel in it. Point to the last letter, the **e**, and say that it has a special job to do. It makes the vowel in the middle of the word say its own name.
- Ask them if they know what that name is. If not tell them we all have a name. The name of the letter a is /ay/.
- Tell them that once the **e** on the end of the word has done its job it is silent, it has nothing more to do.
- In a word like 'name' ask what the **e** has to do, then cover it up and ask them to say the word.
- Do this with several different words before commencing the worksheet activities.

Worksheet activities

Explain that the letter **e** at the end of a word makes the vowel say its own name.

Put letters in a container on each table so that the children can make the words before writing them on the worksheets.

116

Activity 1

- Give the children the worksheet for the long vowel sound and ask them to look at the first picture. What can they see in the picture?
- What sound can they hear at the beginning of the word?
- What sound can they hear in the middle?
- What sound can they hear at the end of the word? Is it the last letter? Why not?
- Go through the rest of the words before children commence the activity.

Activity 2

- **a–e** worksheet: sort the letters into **a–e** words. Write the words in the empty box.
- **i–e** worksheet: build **i–e** words from the given letters. Write the words in the empty box.
- **o–e** worksheet: find the **o–e** words in the wordsearch. Write the words in the empty box. (Words are written up and down as well as across. The initial letter of each word is in bold.)
- **u–e** worksheet: sort the letters into **u–e** words. Write the words in the empty box.

Star word:

- Hold up the star word and ask if anyone knows the word.
- Say the word and ask the children to repeat it.
- Ask them why star words are different. Remind them that they are tricky words; words they have to know by looking at them, not by trying to build them.
- Say sentences with the word 'he' in them. Ask them to make up some for you.
- Hang up the star word and refer back to it at times during each day when you or they use the word, so they hear it in common usage.

Classworks Synthetic Phonics Photocopiable Readers

The following Photocopiable Readers can be used this week:

- the pink bike
- the bike ride
- mike and the mess
- duke and rose
- jane, saba and the doll.

a–e words

he

1.

r __ __ __

c __ __ __

a–e

s __ __ __ __

s __ __ __ __ __

s __ __ __ __

p __ __ __ __

2.

a m e d	List the words you have found
s a c e	
a t e d	
a l e m f	
m a c e	
a n e m	

1. Write **a–e** words for the pictures.   2. Sort the letters and write the correct words in the box.

Classworks: The Synthetic Phonics Book © Helen Hadley, Nelson Thornes Ltd, 2006

i–e words

he

1.

k __ __ __

s __ __ __ __

b __ __ __ __

i–e

b __ __ __

9

n __ __ __

5

f __ __ __

2.

f			List the words you have found
h		d	
m	i	l	e
p		n	
t		v	

1. Write **i–e** words for the pictures.   2. Make words from the letters and write them in the box.

Classworks: The Synthetic Phonics Book © Helen Hadley, Nelson Thornes Ltd, 2006

o–e words

he

1.

c __ __ __

n __ __ __

o–e

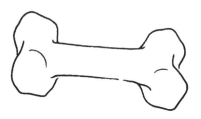

r __ __ __

b __ __ __

s m __ __ __

h __ __ __

2.

t	h	e	m	List the words you have found
b	o	n	e	
e	p	e	t	
t	e	l	l	
r	o	b	e	

1. Write **o–e** words for the pictures.   2. Link letters to make words and write them in the box.

Classworks: The Synthetic Phonics Book © Helen Hadley, Nelson Thornes Ltd, 2006

u–e words

1.

t _ _ _

f l _ _ _

c _ _ _

u–e

m _ _ _

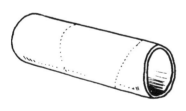

t _ _ _

r _ _ _ _

2.

	List the words you have found
l u e m	
e s u	
b e t u	
u f e s	
l e u r	
t e c u	

1. Write **u–e** words for the pictures.   2. Sort the letters and write the correct words in the box.

Classworks: The Synthetic Phonics Book © Helen Hadley, Nelson Thornes Ltd, 2006

**Week 10
Friday review**

Preparation

- Have ready the laminated cards of letters learnt to date.

Revision

- Holding up each of this week's digraphs in turn, you say, "This is the long vowel sound /ay/. What is it?" The children say the sound.
- The children respond to the sounds as you go through them, getting faster and faster.
- Give out three copies of this week's digraphs, plus all the letters learnt to date, and have a copy of each for yourself.
- Hold up a digraph and ask, "What is this sound?" They respond. "If you have the same sound, hold it up." Do this for all of this week's digraphs several times.
- Say one of this week's sounds and invite someone to come and write it on the board.
- Do this for all of this week's digraphs several times.
- Using the word list, ask the children to come out if they have any of the letters for a word you give them, e.g. hold up the letters for the word 'came'. "What does this word say? Come out if you have any of the letters for the word 'came'."
- Using the word list for reference, say a word and ask the children to come out if they have any of the letters from that word.
- Use the letter fans of letters learnt to date for word building activities – see games and activities, page 5.
- The word lists can also be used to check the progress of individual children.
- Each week, select a few children to check their progress on the minute tracks and to hear them read the zigzag book. You may need to check on some children more frequently than others to ensure they keep up.

This week's word list

cake

made

bite

like

mine

bake

home

nose

cube

tune

he

Building words for pictures

a–e

g _ _ _

c _ _ _

i–e

c _ _ _

k _ _ _

o–e

l _ _ _

n _ _ _

u–e

b _ _ _

m _ _ _

Use long vowels and consonants to complete the words.

Classworks: The Synthetic Phonics Book © Helen Hadley, Nelson Thornes Ltd, 2006

Find the right word

Picture	Words			Picture	Words		
	ripe	pipe	pike		came	cake	came
	cape	ape	tape		side	ride	slide
	rope	dope	mope		cone	bone	code
	cube	tube	tune		tide	hide	bride
	dive	five	hive		lute	bute	flute

1. Say what is in the picture.   2. Read all three words.   3. Circle the right word.

124

Get a Goal

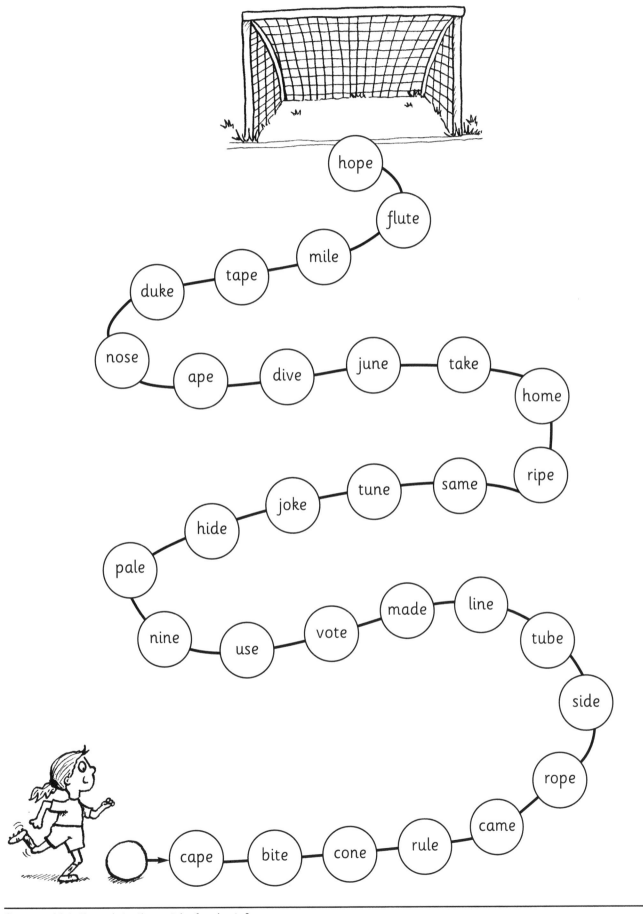

Can you kick them into the net in 1 minute?

Classworks: The Synthetic Phonics Book © Helen Hadley, Nelson Thornes Ltd, 2006

4

I take a bit of
cake to my
dad

5

he is at home
with luke

3

we both had
a bite of cake

6

I hope dad
and luke like
the cake

2

mum bakes a
cake for me
and jane

7

dad and luke
ate the cake

1

Week 10

letters:
a–e, i–e,
o–e, u–e

he

8

no cake was
left on the
plate

Fold across the middle and make a zigzag book.   Sound the letters then read the book.

**Week 11
Lesson plan**

| Monday | *ee* | Tuesday | *ai* | Wednesday | *ay* | Thursday | *oo* |

Follow this sequence to introduce these vowel digraphs: **ee**, **ai**, **ay** and **oo** as in 'moo'.

Identifying the sound

- Hold up items or pictures of items containing the day's vowel digraph.
- Ask the children what the items are.
- What sound is the same in each word?
- Is there anyone in the class whose name has this sound in it? Do they know anyone else whose name has the sound in it?
- Can they think of other words with the day's sound in them?
- Say sentences with some words in them using the day's sound, and ask them to tell you in which words that sound is used.
- Hang up the new vowel digraphs. Use them in daily ten-minute sessions.

Making the sound

Take time to practise the correct way to pronounce each sound with the children.

- /ee/ is made with a wide smiling mouth.
- /ai/ and /ay/ are made in the front of the mouth with the jaw dropped down.
- /oo/ is made in the middle of the mouth through pursed lips.

Learning the sound

- Say it loudly, say it softly, say it rhythmically, say it slowly and then say it quickly several times.
- Hold up or point to pictures of things containing the day's digraph. Emphasise the vowel digraphs, e.g. feeeet – 'feet' etc.
- Keep vowel digraphs long and the consonants short.

Worksheet activities

Put letters in a container on each table so that the children can make the words before writing them on the worksheets.

Activity 1
- Give the children the worksheet for the vowel digraph and ask them to look at the first picture. What can they see in the picture?
- What vowel sound can they hear in the word?
- Go through the rest of the words before children commence the activity.

Activity 2
- **ee**, **ai** and **oo** worksheets: build words from the given letters. Write the words in the empty box.
- **ay** worksheet: find the **ay** words in the wordsearch. Write the words in the empty box. (Words are written up and down as well as across. The initial letter of each word is in bold.)

Star word:

- Hold up the star word and ask if anyone knows the word.
- Say the word and ask the children to repeat it.
- Ask them why star words are different. Remind them that they are tricky words; words they have to know by looking at them, not by trying to build them.
- Say sentences with the word 'we' in them. Ask them to make up some for you.
- Hang up the star word and refer back to it at times during each day when you or they use the word, so they hear it in common usage.

Classworks Synthetic Phonics Photocopiable Readers

The following Photocopiable Readers can be used this week:

- scoop the dog
- sam the snail
- jay and the black paint
- the clay doll
- a bag of sweets.

ee words

we

1.

f _ _ _

t r _ _

s h _ _ _ _

ee

t _ _ _ _ _

b _ _

s l _ _ _ _

2.

b			List the words you have found
f		l	
p	ee		
sh		p	
sl		t	
sw			

1. Write **ee** words for the pictures.   2. Make words from the letters and write them in the box.

Classworks: The Synthetic Phonics Book © Helen Hadley, Nelson Thornes Ltd, 2006

ai words

we

1.

s __ __ __

t __ __ __

s n __ __ __

ai

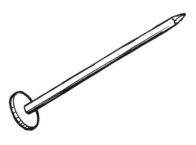

n __ __ __

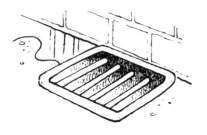

d r __ __ __

p __ __ __

2.

	List the words you have found
ʃ	
m l	
p ai n	
r nt	
tr	

1. Write **ai** words for the pictures.   2. Make words from the letters and write them in the box.

Classworks: The Synthetic Phonics Book © Helen Hadley, Nelson Thornes Ltd, 2006

ay words

we

1.

s __ __ __ __

p __ __

p __ __ __

ay

b __ __

l __ __

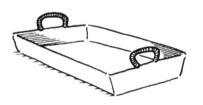

t __ __ __

2.

d	m	a	y
a	s	**a**	y
y	e	t	**b**
a	l	e	a
p	l	a	y

List the words you have found

---

1. Write **ay** words for the pictures.   2. Link letters to make words and write them in the box.

Classworks: The Synthetic Phonics Book © Helen Hadley, Nelson Thornes Ltd, 2006

oo words

1.

m __ __ __   b __ __ __ __

oo

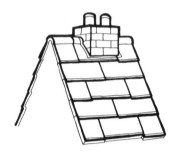

s p __ __ __   r __ __ __ __

b __ __ __   h __ __ __

2.

b f	
m m	List the words you have found
r oo n	
sh t	
sp	

1. Write **oo** words for the pictures.   2. Make words from the letters and write them in the box.

Classworks: The Synthetic Phonics Book © Helen Hadley, Nelson Thornes Ltd, 2006

Week 11
Friday review

Preparation

- Have ready the laminated cards of letters learnt to date.

Revision

- Holding up each of this week's digraphs in turn, you say, "This is **ee**. What is it?" The children say the sound.
- The children respond to the digraphs as you go through them, getting faster and faster.
- Give out three copies of this week's digraphs, plus all the letters learnt to date, and have a copy of each for yourself.
- Hold up a digraph and ask, "What is this sound?" They respond. "If you have the same sound, hold it up." Do this for all of this week's digraphs several times.
- Say one of this week's sounds and invite someone to come and write it on the board.
- Do this for all of this week's digraphs several times.
- Using the word list, ask the children to come out if they have any of the letters for a word you give them, e.g. hold up the letters for the word 'peep'. "What does this word say? Come out if you have any of the letters for the word 'peep'."
- Using the word list for reference, say a word and ask the children to come out if they have any of the letters from that word.
- Use the letter fans of letters learnt to date for word building activities – see games and activities, page 5.
- The word lists can also be used to check the progress of individual children.
- Each week, select a few children to check their progress on the minute tracks and to hear them read the zigzag book. You may need to check on some children more frequently than others to ensure they keep up.

This week's word list

peep

cheek

sweet

pail

snail

day

play

broom

hoop

spoon

we

Building words for pictures

ee

b _ _

b r _ _ _

ai

r _ _ _

s p r _ _

ay

f _ _ _

s n _ _ _

oo

t _ _ _

b _ _ _ _

Use vowel digraphs and consonants to complete the words.

Classworks: The Synthetic Phonics Book © Helen Hadley, Nelson Thornes Ltd, 2006

Find the right word

Picture	Words		Picture	Words
	seed steel sweet			 nail snail sail
	pain paint rain		**3**	cheek steep three
	spoon spoof soon			 shoot hoot hoof
	pray say spray			 pay say bay
	three teeth meet			 loop noon moon

135

1. Say what is in the picture.   2. Read all three words.   3. Circle the right word.

Classworks: The Synthetic Phonics Book © Helen Hadley, Nelson Thornes Ltd, 2006

Party-time

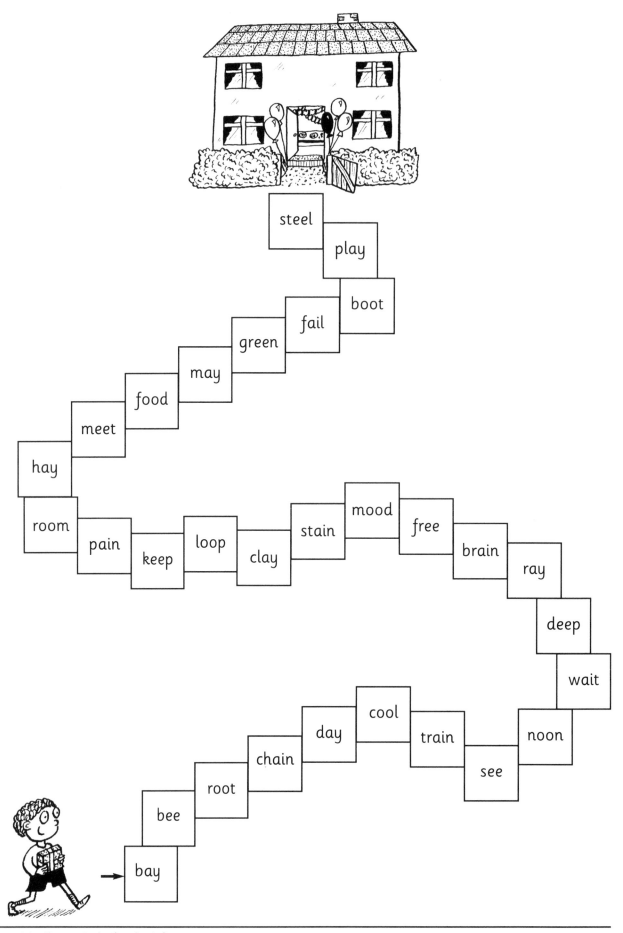

Can you get to the party in 1 minute?

Classworks: The Synthetic Phonics Book © Helen Hadley, Nelson Thornes Ltd, 2006

he trod on
his train and
broke it

4

jools has had
a bad day.
he is cross

3

ray and I
went to see
jools

2

Week 11
letters:
ee, ai, ay, oo

we

1

let's go and
see if my dad
can mend it

5

dad came
down from
the roof to
see jools'
train

6

dad mended
jools' train

7

we had fun
with jools'
train

8

Fold across the middle and make a zigzag book.   Sound the letters then read the book.

Classworks: *The Synthetic Phonics Book* © Helen Hadley, Nelson Thornes Ltd, 2006

**Week 12
Lesson plan**

| Monday | **oa** | Tuesday | **oi** | Wednesday | **ou** | Thursday | **ow** |

Follow this sequence to introduce these vowel digraphs: **oa**, **oi**, **ou** and **ow** as in 'owl'.

Identifying the sound

- Hold up items or pictures of items containing the day's vowel digraph.
- Ask the children what the items are.
- What sound is the same in each word?
- Is there anyone in the class whose name has this sound in it? Do they know anyone else whose name has the sound in it?
- Can they think of other words with the day's sound in them?
- Say sentences with some words in them using the day's sound, and ask them to tell you in which words that sound is used.
- Hang up the new vowel digraphs. Use them in daily ten-minute sessions.

Making the sound

Take time to practise the correct way to pronounce each sound with the children.

- /oa/ is made with an open mouth closing to a pout – as in the 'oh' of 'oh dear'.
- /oi/ is made in the front of the mouth with the mouth in an oval shape widening to a smile.
- /ou/ and /ow/ are made with a wide open mouth closing to a pout – as if someone had pinched them.

Learning the sound

- Say it loudly, say it softly, say it rhythmically, say it slowly and then say it quickly several times.
- Hold up or point to pictures of things containing the day's digraph.
- Keep vowel digraphs long and the consonants short.

Worksheet activities

Put letters in a container on each table so that the children can make the words before writing them on the worksheets.

Activity 1
- Give the children the worksheet for the vowel digraph and ask them to look at the first picture. What can they see in the picture?
- What vowel sound can they hear in the word?
- Go through the rest of the words before the children commence the activity.

Activity 2
- **oa** and **ou** worksheets: build words from the given letters. Write the words in the box.
- **oi** and **ow** worksheets: find the **oi** or **ow** words in the wordsearch. Write the words in the box. (Words are written up and down as well as across. The initial letter of each word is in bold.)

Star word:

- Hold up the star word and ask if anyone knows the word.
- Say the word and ask the children to repeat it.
- Ask them why star words are different. Remind them that they are tricky words; words they have to know by looking at them, not by trying to build them.
- Say sentences with the word 'she' in them. Ask them to make up some for you.
- Hang up the star word and refer back to it at times during each day when you or they use the word, so they hear it in common usage.

Classworks Synthetic Phonics Photocopiable Readers

The following Photocopiable Readers can be used this week:

- joan and rex
- roy and boyd
- the pink crab
- the owl in the tree
- the clowns.

oa words

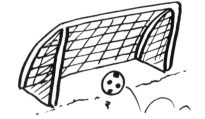

she

1.

g _ _ _   l _ _ _

oa

g _ _ _   f _ _ _

c _ _ _   b _ _ _

2.

b		k	List the words you have found
c		p	
g	oa		
s		st	
t		t	

1. Write **oa** words for the pictures.   2. Make words from the letters and write them in the box.

Classworks: The Synthetic Phonics Book © Helen Hadley, Nelson Thornes Ltd, 2006

oi words

she

1.

c __ __ __ __

__ __ l

oi

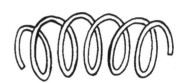

p __ __ __ __

c __ __ __ __

b __ __ __

j __ __ __ __

2.

a	j	o	i	n	List the words you have found
m	o	i	s	t	
i	l	l	o	a	
e	b	o	i	l	
c	o	i	l	e	
j	o	i	n	t	

1. Write **oi** words for the pictures.   2. Link letters to make words and write them in the box.

ou words

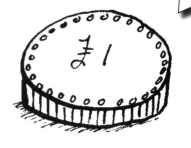

1.

s c __ __ __   p __ __ __ __

ou

s n __ __ __   c l __ __ __

   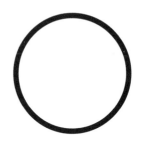

m __ __ __ __   r __ __ __ __

2.

b	d	List the words you have found
l	nd	
p ou		
s	t	
sh	th	

1. Write **ou** words for the pictures.   2. Make words from the letters and write them in the box.

ow words

she

1.

o __ __

d __ __ __

c __ __ __ __

ow

f __ __ __ __

c __ __

c __ __ __ __

2.

c	o	w	b	d	List the words you have found
l	n	e	r	o	
o	l	h	o	w	
w	t	o	w	n	
n	o	w	n	s	
g	r	o	w	l	

1. Write **ow** words for the pictures.   2. Link letters to make words and write them in the box.

Classworks: The Synthetic Phonics Book © Helen Hadley, Nelson Thornes Ltd, 2006

143

Week 12
Friday review

Preparation

- Have ready the laminated cards of letters learnt to date.

Revision

- Holding up each of this week's digraphs in turn, you say, "This is **oa**. What is it?" The children say the sound.
- The children respond to the digraphs as you go through them, getting faster and faster.
- Give out three copies of this week's digraphs, plus all the letters learnt to date, and have a copy of each for yourself.
- Hold up a digraph and ask, "What is this sound?" They respond. "If you have the same sound, hold it up." Do this for all of this week's digraphs several times.
- Say one of this week's sounds and invite someone to come and write it on the board.
- Do this for all of this week's digraphs several times.
- Using the word list, ask the children to come out if they have any of the letters for a word you give them, e.g. hold up the letters for the word 'coat'. "What does this word say? Come out if you have any of the letters for the word 'coat'."
- Using the word list for reference, say a word and ask the children to come out if they have any of the letters from that word.
- Use the letter fans of letters learnt to date for word building activities – see games and activities, page 5.
- The word lists can also be used to check the progress of individual children.
- Each week, select a few children to check their progress on the minute tracks and to hear them read the zigzag book. You may need to check on some children more frequently than others to ensure they keep up.

This week's word list

coat	count
goal	mouth
loaf	brown
boil	clown
point	she
shout	

Building words for pictures

oa

l _ _ _

c l _ _ _

oi

c _ _ _ _

m _ _ _

ou

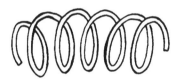

c _ _

c _ _ _

ow

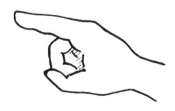

p _ _ _ _

c l _ _ _ _

Use vowel digraphs and consonants to complete words.

Find the right word

	owl cowl fowl	coat moat boat
	load road toad	joy boy roy
	boy coy toy	point joint coin
	foil coil boil	loud bound cloud
	mound mouth south	down clown town

1. Say what is in the picture.　　2. Read all three words.　　3. Circle the right word.

Classworks: The Synthetic Phonics Book © Helen Hadley Nelson Thornes Ltd 2006

Run the track

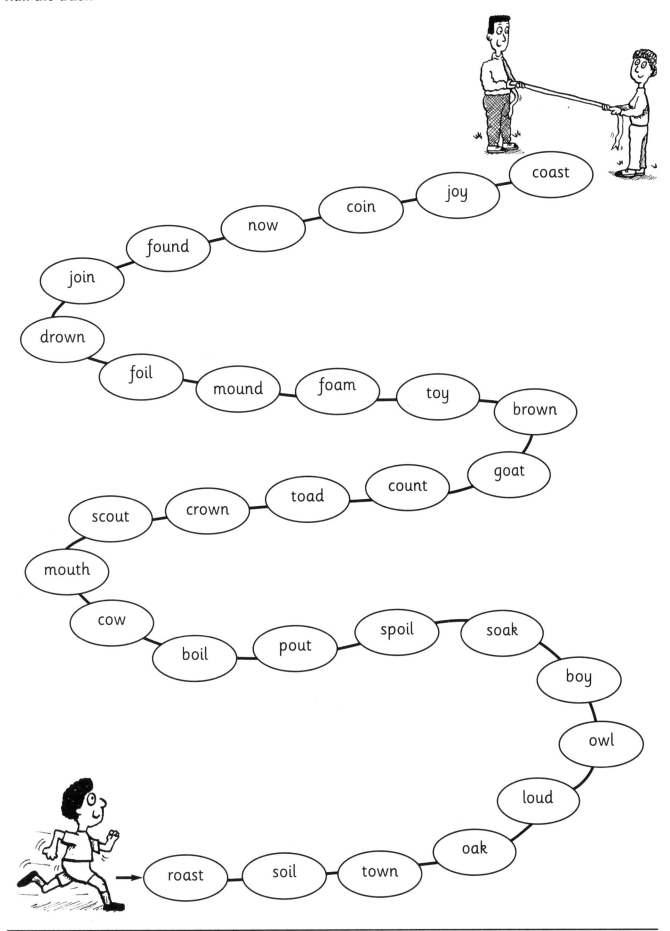

coast

joy

coin

now

found

join

drown

foil

mound

foam

toy

brown

goat

count

toad

crown

scout

mouth

cow

boil

pout

spoil

soak

boy

owl

loud

oak

roast

soil

town

Can you reach the tape in 1 minute?

Classworks: The Synthetic Phonics Book © Helen Hadley, Nelson Thornes Ltd, 2006

we went on
the coach to
see gran

5

we ran down
the road to
catch the
coach

4

she had some
toys for us

she
them out on
we play with

the grass

7

my mate ray
came to my
home

2

Week 12
letters: oa, oi,
oy, ou, ow

she

1

she let us
take them
back home
with us

8

Fold across the middle and make a zigzag book.   Sound the letters then read the book.

Classworks: The Synthetic Phonics Book © Helen Hadley Nelson Thornes Ltd 2006

148

**Week 13
Lesson plan**

said

| Monday | **ea** | Tuesday | **oo** | Wednesday | **aw** | Thursday | **ow** |

Follow this sequence to introduce these vowel digraphs: **ea**, **oo** as in 'book', **aw** and **ow** as in 'glow'.

Identifying the sound

- Hold up items or pictures of items containing the day's vowel digraph.
- Ask the children what the items are.
- What sound is the same in each word?
- Is there anyone in the class whose name has this sound in it? Do they know anyone else whose name has the sound in it?
- Can they think of other words with the day's sound in them?
- Say sentences with some words in them using the day's sound, and ask them to tell you in which words that sound is used.
- Hang up the new vowel digraphs. Use them in daily ten-minute sessions.

Making the sound

Take time to practise the correct way to pronounce each sound with the children.

- /ea/ is made with a wide smiling mouth.
- /oo/ is made in the front of the mouth through pursed lips.
- /aw/ is made with the lips pushed forwards.
- /ow/ is made with an open mouth closing to a pout – as in saying the word 'oh'.

Learning the sound

- Say it loudly, say it softly, say it rhythmically, say it slowly and then say it quickly several times.
- Hold up or point to pictures of things containing the day's digraph.
- Keep long vowel digraphs long and the consonants short.

Worksheet activities

Put letters in a container on each table so that the children can make the words before writing them on the worksheets.

Activity 1
- Give the children the worksheet for the vowel digraph and ask them to look at the first picture. What can they see in the picture?
- What vowel sound can they hear in the word?
- Go through the rest of the words before the children commence the activity.

Activity 2
- **ea** and **ow** worksheets: sort the letters into words. Write the words in the box.
- **oo** and **aw** worksheets: build words from the given letters. Write the words in the box.

Star word:

- Hold up the star word and ask if anyone knows the word.
- Say the word and ask the children to repeat it.
- Ask them why star words are different. Remind them that they are tricky words; words they have to know by looking at them, not by trying to build them.
- Say sentences with the word 'said' in them. Ask them to make up some for you.
- Hang up the star word and refer back to it at times during each day when you or they use the word, so they hear it in common usage.

Classworks Synthetic Phonics Photocopiable Readers

The following Photocopiable Readers can be used this week:

- help! help!
- the boys go to camp
- bea's gift
- dean, the rook and the book
- bea and the hawk.

ea words

said

1.

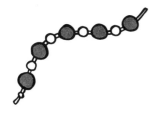

b __ __ __ __   m __ __ __

ea

c __ __ __ __   s __ __ __ __

l __ __ __   b __ __ __ __ __

2.

	List the words you have found
m n e a	
h c e a	
c h a e p	
r d a e m	
s k e a p	
r t t a e	

1. Write **ea** words for the pictures.   2. Sort the letters and write the correct words in the box.

oo words

said

1.

f __ __ __

b __ __ __

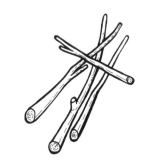

oo

w __ __ __

c __ __ __

h __ __ __

h __ __ __

2.

c h l oo r k t sh	List the words you have found

1. Write **oo** words for the pictures.   2. Make words from the letters and write them in the box.

Classworks: The Synthetic Phonics Book © Helen Hadley, Nelson Thornes Ltd, 2006

aw words

said

1.

p __ __

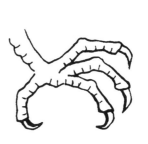

c _ _ _

s __ __ __ __

aw

y __ __ __

s __ __

s __ __ __ __

2.

		List the words you have found
d		
f	l	
l	aw	
p	n	
r		
sh		

1. Write **aw** words for the pictures.   2. Make words from the letters and write them in the box.

ow words

said

1.

s __ __ __

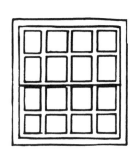

w __ __ __ __ __

t __ __ __ __

ow

b __ __ __

m __ __

b __ __ __

2.

r o w c	List the words you have found
s w o l	
h o w s	
w o r	
t o w r h	
l o w g	

1. Write **ow** words for the pictures.   2. Sort the letters and write the correct words in the box.

Classworks: The Synthetic Phonics Book © Helen Hadley, Nelson Thornes Ltd, 2006

Week 13
Friday review

Preparation

- Have ready the laminated cards of letters learnt to date.

Revision

- Holding up each of this week's digraphs in turn, you say, "This is **ea**, a long /ee/ sound. What is it?" The children say the sound.
- The children respond to the digraphs as you go through them, getting faster and faster.
- Give out three copies of this week's digraphs, plus all the letters learnt to date, and have a copy of each for yourself.
- Hold up a digraph and ask, "What is this sound?" They respond. "If you have the same sound, hold it up." Do this for all of this week's digraphs several times.
- Say one of this week's sounds and invite someone to come and write it on the board.
- Do this for all of this week's digraphs several times.
- Using the word list, ask the children to come out if they have any of the letters for a word you give them, e.g. hold up the letters for the word 'bead'. "What does this word say? Come out if you have any of the letters for the word 'bead'."
- Using the word list for reference, say a word and ask the children to come out if they have any of the letters from that word.
- Use the letter fans of letters learnt to date for word building activities – see games and activities, page 5.
- The word lists can also be used to check the progress of individual children.
- Each week, select a few children to check their progress on the minute tracks and to hear them read the zigzag book. You may need to check on some children more frequently than others to ensure they keep up.

This week's word list

bead	claw
leaf	draw
team	show
book	throw
took	said
hood	

Complete the words

ea

c l __ __   b __ __ __

oo

b __ __ __ __   b l __ __

aw

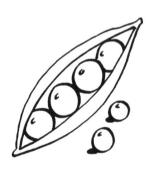

t h r __ __   p __ __ __

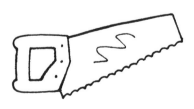

ow

s __ __   h __ __ __

Use vowel digraphs and consonants to complete the words.

Classworks: The Synthetic Phonics Book © Helen Hadley, Nelson Thornes Ltd, 2006

Find the right word

Picture	Words	Picture	Words
	shook hook look		neat beat seat
	crow glow throw		took cook look
	claw draw law		show flow blow
	heat meat leaf		pawn paw jaw
	nook rook book		bean beat bead

1. Say what is in the picture.   2. Read all three words.   3. Circle the right word.

Classworks: The Synthetic Phonics Book © Helen Hadley, Nelson Thornes Ltd, 2006

Get a Goal

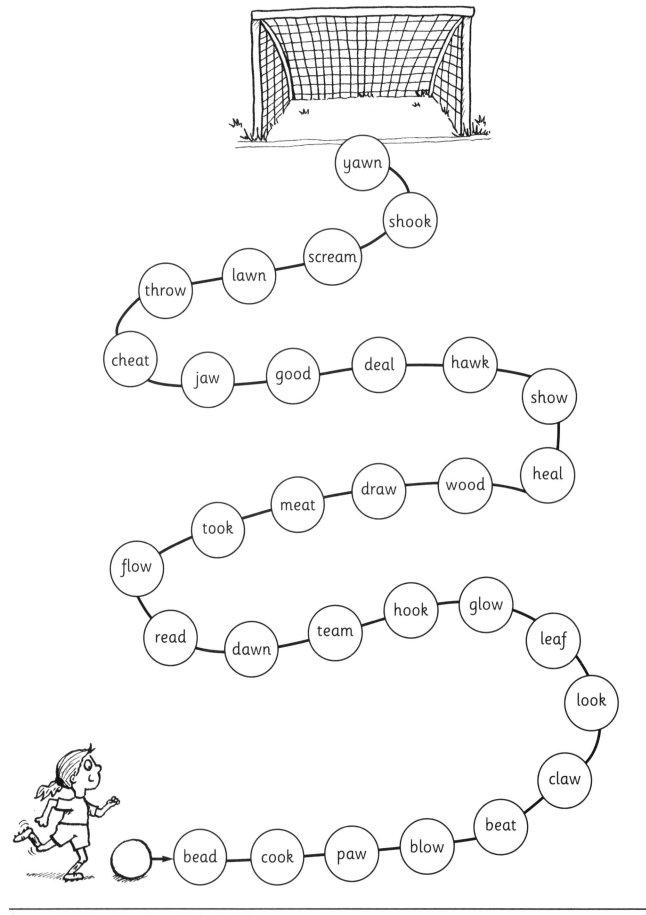

Can you kick them into the net in 1 minute?

Classworks: The Synthetic Phonics Book © Helen Hadley, Nelson Thornes Ltd, 2006

we made foot
prints in the
sand

4

the sun is out.
it is a fine
day

3

mum said we
will take
brook the
dog to the
coast

2

Week 13

letters:
ea, oo, aw,
ow

said

1

the dog made
paw prints in
the sand

5

I went out in
a boat with
my dad

6

we got some
fish on a
hook

7

mum said she
will cook the
fish for tea

8

Fold across the middle and make a zigzag book.   Sound the letters then read the book.

Classworks: The Synthetic Phonics Book © Helen Hadley, Nelson Thornes Ltd, 2006

159

**Week 14
Lesson plan**

Monday	**ar**	Tuesday	**ir**	Wednesday	**or**	Thursday	**ur**

Follow this sequence to introduce these digraphs: **ar**, **ir**, **or** and **ur**.

Identifying the sound

- Hold up items or pictures of items containing the day's digraph.
- Ask the children what the items are.
- What sound is the same in each word?
- Is there anyone in the class whose name has this sound in it? Do they know anyone else whose name has the sound in it?
- Can they think of other words with the day's sound in them?
- Say sentences with some words in them using the day's sound, and ask them to tell you in which words that sound is used.
- Hang up the new digraphs. Use them in daily ten-minute sessions.

Making the sound

Take time to practise the correct way to pronounce each sound with the children.

- /ar/ is made with a wide open mouth.
- /ir/ and /ur/ are made by pushing forward the lower jaw.
- /or/ is made with the lips pushed forwards.

Learning the sound

- Say it loudly, say it softly, say it rhythmically, say it slowly and then say it quickly several times.
- Hold up or point to pictures of things containing the day's digraph.
- Keep digraphs long and the consonants short.

Worksheet activities

Put letters in a container on each table so that the children can make the words before writing them on the worksheets.

Activity 1
- Give the children the worksheet for the digraph and ask them to look at the first picture. What can they see in the picture?
- What vowel sound can they hear in the word?
- Go through the rest of the words before the children commence the activity.

Activity 2
- **ar** and **or** worksheets: build words from the given letters. Write the words in the box.
- **ir** worksheet: sort the letters into words. Write the words in the box.
- **ur** worksheet: find the **ur** words in the wordsearch. Write the words in the box. (Words are written up and down as well as across. The initial letter of each word is in bold.)

Star word:

- Hold up the star word and ask if anyone knows the word.
- Say the word and ask the children to repeat it.

- Ask them why star words are different. Remind them that they are tricky words; words they have to know by looking at them, not by trying to build them.
- Say sentences with the word 'they' in them. Ask them to make up some for you.
- Hang up the star word and refer back to it at times during each day when you or they use the word, so they hear it in common usage.

Classworks Synthetic Phonics Photocopiable Readers

The following Photocopiable Readers can be used this week:

- a day at the beach
- the boys in the barn
- the girl in the park
- a trip to the zoo
- lorna's dog.

ar words

they

1.

s __ __ __ __

s __ __ __

ar

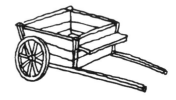

c __ __

d __ __ __

c __ __ __

s __ __ __ __

2.

b		k
d		m
h	ar	n
p		p
sh		t

List the words you have found

---

1. Write **ar** words for the pictures.   2. Make words from the letters and write them in the box.

Classworks: The Synthetic Phonics Book © Helen Hadley, Nelson Thornes Ltd, 2006

162

ir words

they

1.

b __ __ __

s __ __ __ __

s k __ __ __

ir

s t __ __

g __ __ __

f __ __

2.

	List the words you have found
r i f	
i r t d	
d i r b	
l i r g	
i r t s	
m f i r	

1. Write **ir** words for the pictures.   2. Sort the letters and write the correct words in the box.

Classworks: The Synthetic Phonics Book © Helen Hadley, Nelson Thornes Ltd, 2006

or words

they

1.

c _ _ _

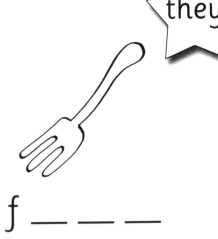

f _ _ _

s h _ _ _

or

t _ _ _ _

f _ _ _

c _ _ _ _

2.

c		d	List the words you have found
f		k	
p	or	m	
sh		n	
st		t	

1. Write **or** words for the pictures.   2. Make words from the letters and write them in the box.

Classworks: The Synthetic Phonics Book © Helen Hadley, Nelson Thornes Ltd, 2006

164

ur words

they

1.

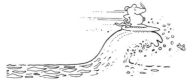

s _ _ _

b _ _ _ _

c h _ _ _ _

ur

f _ _

c _ _ _

h _ _ _

2.

s	p	u	r	t	List the words you have found
u	**u**	s	e	**h**	
r	r	**f**	a	u	
f	l	u	d	r	
b	u	r	s	t	

1. Write **ur** words for the pictures.   2. Link letters to make words and write them in the box.

Classworks: The Synthetic Phonics Book © Helen Hadley, Nelson Thornes Ltd, 2006

165

Week 14
Friday review

Preparation

- Have ready the laminated cards of letters learnt to date.

Revision

- Holding up each of this week's digraphs in turn, you say, "This is **ar**. What is it?" The children say the sound.
- The children respond to the digraphs as you go through them, getting faster and faster.
- Give out three copies of this week's digraphs, plus all the letters learnt to date, and have a copy of each for yourself.
- Hold up a digraph and ask, "What is this sound?" They respond. "If you have the same sound, hold it up." Do this for all of this week's digraphs several times.
- Say one of this week's sounds and invite someone to come and write it on the board.
- Do this for all of this week's digraphs several times.
- Using the word list, ask the children to come out if they have any of the letters for a word you give them, e.g. hold up the letters for the word 'cart'. "What does this word say? Come out if you have any of the letters for the word 'cart'."
- Using the word list for reference, say a word and ask the children to come out if they have any of the letters from that word.
- Use the letter fans of letters learnt to date for word building activities – see games and activities, page 5.
- The word lists can also be used to check the progress of individual children.
- Each week, select a few children to check their progress on the minute tracks and to hear them read the zigzag book. You may need to check on some children more frequently than others to ensure they keep up.

This week's word list

cart	cord
star	sports
park	curl
girl	hurt
bird	they
fork	

166

Complete the words

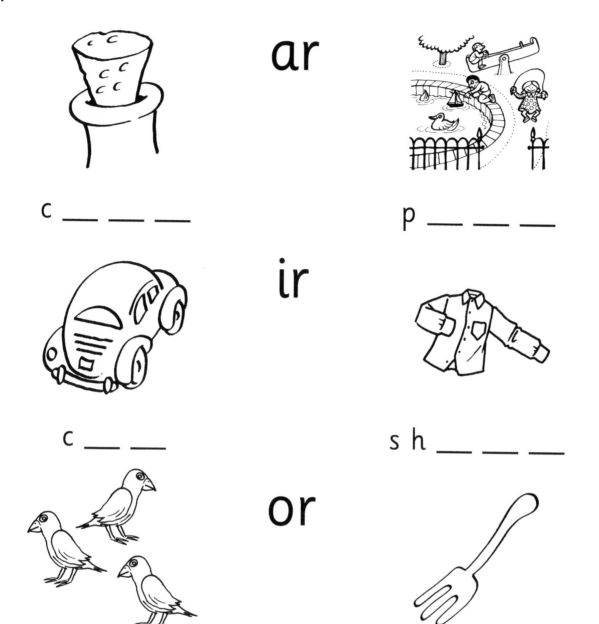

ar

c _ _ _

p _ _ _

ir

c _ _

s h _ _ _

or

b _ _ _ s

f _ _ _

ur

b _ _ _ _

c _ _ _ _

Use vowel digraphs and consonants to complete the words.

Find the right word

	skirt shirt stir		cord ford corn
	barn hark bark		furl hurl curl
	ford cork fork		car bar far
	bird birth dirt		firm bird fir
	fort for port		scar scarf cart

1. Say what is in the picture. 2. Read all three words. 3. Circle the right word.

Classworks *The Synthetic Phonics Book* © Helen Hadley Nelson Thornes Ltd 2006

Party-time

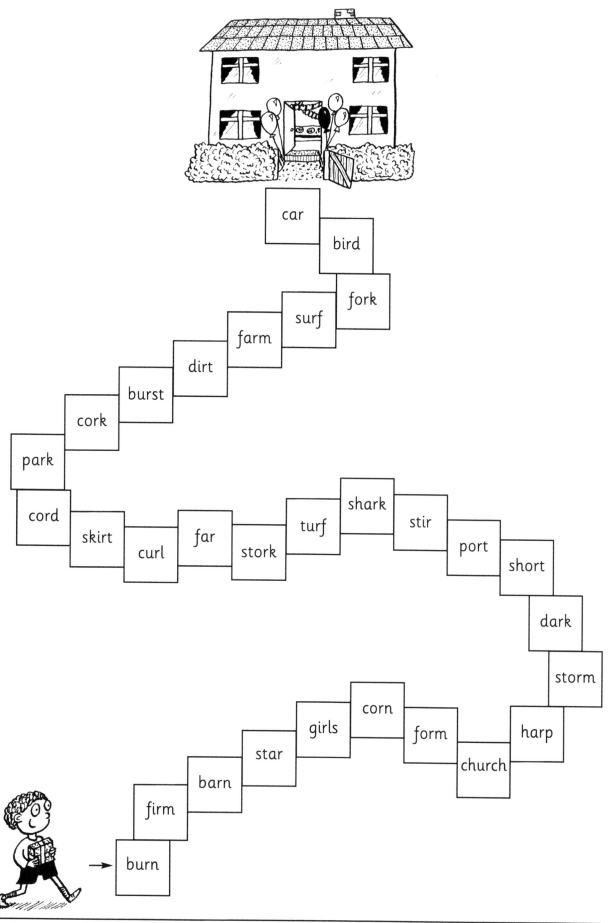

Can you get to the party in 1 minute?

Classworks: The Synthetic Phonics Book © Helen Hadley, Nelson Thornes Ltd, 2006

they started
to bark at
the ducks

4

we ran to get
away from
the ducks

5

the dogs ran
to the pond

3

we held the
dogs' fur and
put leads on
them

6

karl and I
took the dogs
to the park

2

karl said we
must take the
dogs back
home

7

Week 14

letters:
ar, ir, or, ur

they

1

his shirt and
my short skirt
had lots of
mud on them

8

Fold across the middle and make a zigzag book.   Sound the letters then read the book.

170

**Week 15
Lesson plan**

| Monday | er | Tuesday | ight | Wednesday | y | Thursday | ew |

Follow this sequence to introduce the letters or letter clusters: **er**, **igh**, **y** and **ew**.

Identifying the sound

- Hold up items or pictures of items containing the day's sound.
- Ask the children what the items are.
- What sound is the same in each word?
- Is there anyone in the class whose name has this sound in it? Do they know anyone else whose name has the sound in it?
- Can they think of other words with the day's sound in them?
- Say sentences with some words in them using the day's sound, and ask them to tell you in which words that sound is used.
- Hang up the new letters or letter clusters. Use them in daily ten-minute sessions.

Making the sound

Take time to practise the correct way to pronounce each sound with the children.

- /er/ is made by pushing forward the lower jaw.
- /igh/ and /ight/ are made by dropping the lower jaw – almost closing it and flicking the tongue against the roof of the mouth for the /t/.
- /ew/ is made at the front of the mouth with the lips pushed forwards.

Learning the sound

- Say it loudly, say it softly, say it rhythmically, say it slowly and then say it quickly several times.
- Hold up or point to pictures of things containing the day's sound.
- Keep vowel sounds long and the consonants short.

Worksheet activities

Put letters in a container on each table so that the children can make the words before writing them on the worksheets.

Activity 1
- Give the children the worksheet for the sound and ask them to look at the first picture. What can they see in the picture?
- What sound can they hear in the word?
- Go through the rest of the words before the children commence the activity.

Activity 2
- **er** and **y** worksheets: build words from the given letters. Write the words in the box.
- **igh** worksheet: sort the letters into words. Write the words in the box.
- **ew** worksheet: find the **ew** words in the wordsearch. Write the words in the box. (Words are written up and down as well as across. The initial letter of each word is in bold.)

Star word:

- Hold up the star word and ask if anyone knows the word.
- Say the word and ask the children to repeat it.
- Ask them why star words are different. Remind them that they are tricky words; words they have to know by looking at them, not by trying to build them.
- Say sentences with the word 'me' in them. Ask them to make up some for you.
- Hang up the star word and refer back to it at times during each day when you or they use the word, so they hear it in common usage.

Classworks Synthetic Phonics Photocopiable Readers

The following Photocopiable Readers can be used this week:

- the flight to spain
- the witch, her cat and her hat
- the lost bag
- let's feed the birds
- down on the farm.

er words

me

1.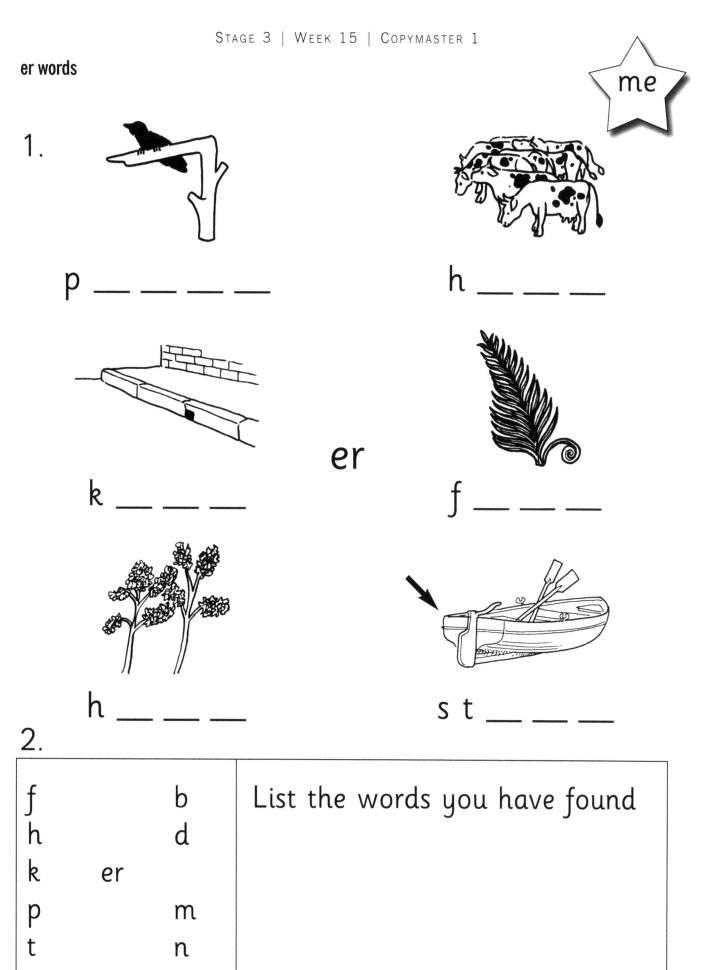

p _ _ _ _

h _ _ _

er

k _ _ _

f _ _ _

h _ _ _

s t _ _ _

2.

f		b	List the words you have found
h		d	
k	er		
p		m	
t		n	

1. Write **er** words for the pictures.   2. Make words from the letters and write them in the box.

Classworks: The Synthetic Phonics Book © Helen Hadley, Nelson Thornes Ltd, 2006

igh words

me

1.

n _ _ _ t

l _ _ _ t

t _ _ _ t s

igh

f _ _ _ _ t

2 + 2 = 4 ✓

r _ _ _ t

f _ _ _ t

2.

	List the words you have found
i g h t t	
t i g h r	
t h i g s	
b r i h t g	
t h m i g	
i g h t f r	
h i g l t	

1. Write **igh** words for the pictures. 2. Sort the letters and write the correct words in the box.

Classworks: The Synthetic Phonics Book © Helen Hadley, Nelson Thornes Ltd, 2006

y words

me

1.

s __ __

c __ __

s __ __

y

f __ __

f __ __

d __ __

2.

	k		List the words you have found
d	l		
f		y	
	p		
s			
t	r		

1. Write **y** words for the pictures.   2. Make words from the letters and write them in the box.

Classworks: The Synthetic Phonics Book © Helen Hadley, Nelson Thornes Ltd, 2006

ew words

1.

c _ _ _

n _ _ s

n _ _

ew

s c _ _ _

g r _ _

c h _ _

2.

u	**g**	**n**	e	t	List the words you have found
c	r	e	w	**c**	
m	e	w	a	h	
s	w	s	h	e	
s	c	r	e	w	

1. Write **ew** words for the pictures.   2. Link letters to make words and write them in the box.

Classworks: The Synthetic Phonics Book © Helen Hadley, Nelson Thornes Ltd, 2006

Week 15
Friday review

Preparation

- Have ready the laminated cards of letters learnt to date.

Revision

- Holding up each of this week's sounds in turn, you say, "This is **er**. What is it?" The children say the sound.
- The children respond to the sounds as you go through them, getting faster and faster.
- Give out three copies of this week's sounds, plus all the letters learnt to date, and have a copy of each for yourself.
- Hold up a sound and ask, "What is this sound?" They respond. "If you have the same sound, hold it up." Do this for all of this week's sounds several times.
- Say one of this week's sounds and invite someone to come and write it on the board.
- Do this for all of this week's sounds several times.
- Using the word list, ask the children to come out if they have any of the letters for a word you give them, e.g. hold up the letters for the word 'fern'. "What does this word say? Come out if you have any of the letters for the word 'fern'."
- Using the word list for reference, say a word and ask the children to come out if they have any of the letters from that word.
- Use the letter fans of letters learnt to date for word building activities – see games and activities, page 5.
- The word lists can also be used to check the progress of individual children.
- Each week, select a few children to check their progress on the minute tracks and to hear them read the zigzag book. You may need to check on some children more frequently than others to ensure they keep up.

This week's word list

fern

herd

light

sight

bright

my

fly

spy

crew

grew

me

Building words for pictures

er

f __ __

n __ __ __ __

ight

k __ __ __

d r __ __

y

l __ __ __ __

p __ __ __ __

ew

s c r __ __

c __ __

Use digraphs and consonants to complete words.

Classworks: The Synthetic Phonics Book © Helen Hadley, Nelson Thornes Ltd, 2006

Find the right word

	pert	perch perm
	spy	fly shy
	flight	fight might
	spew	chew screw
	sight	bight right

	bright night light
	flew chew blew
	fern stern term
	fly sky shy
	kerb herd her

1. Say what is in the picture.   2. Read all three words.   3. Circle the right word.

Classworks: The Synthetic Phonics Book © Helen Hadley, Nelson Thornes Ltd, 2006

Run the Track

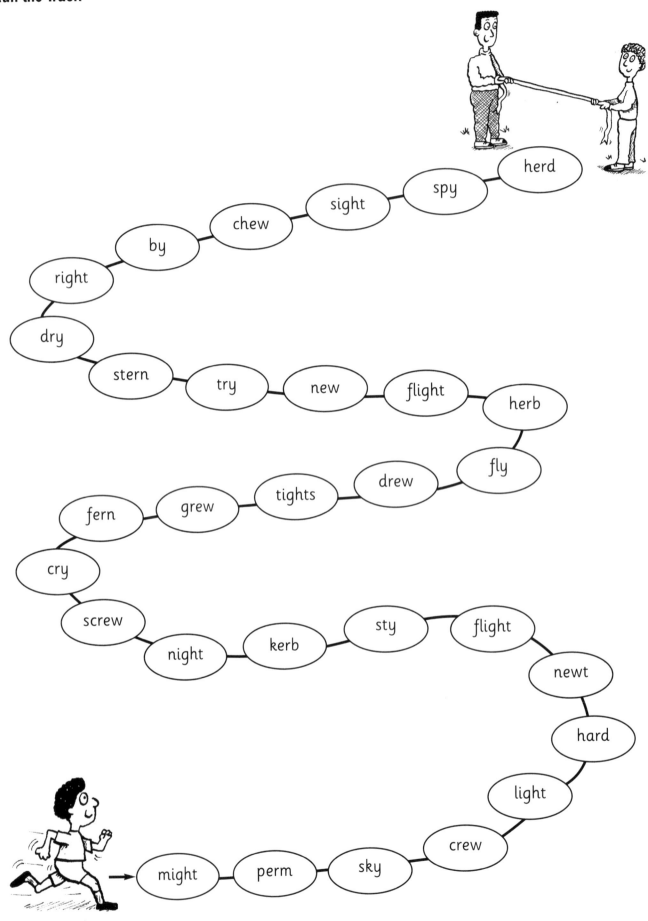

herd

spy

sight

chew

by

right

dry

stern

try

new

flight

herb

fly

drew

tights

grew

fern

cry

screw

night

kerb

sty

flight

newt

hard

light

crew

might

perm

sky

Can you reach the tape in 1 minute?

Classworks: The Synthetic Phonics Book © Helen Hadley, Nelson Thornes Ltd, 2006

the plane
took a long
time to fly to
spain

4

it took us to
the airport

3

the car was
at the kerb
for mum and
me

2

Week 15
letters:
er, ight, y, ew

we had a
great time in
spain then
flew home

me

1

mum and I
went to bed
late that
night

5

the next day
the sun was
bright so we
went to the
beach

6

mum said we
might get
burnt so she
spread sun
cream on me

7

8

181

Fold across the middle and make a zigzag book.   Sound the letters then read the book.

Classworks: The Synthetic Phonics Book © Helen Hadley, Nelson Thornes Ltd, 2006